THE REAL READER'S QUARTERLY

Slightly Foxed

'Asking the Right Questions'

NO. 65   SPRING 2020

Editors Gail Pirkis & Hazel Wood
Marketing and publicity Stephanie Allen & Jennie Harrison Bunning
Bookshops Anna Kirk
Subscriptions Hattie Summers & Jess Dalby

Cover illustration: Kelly Louise Judd, 'Spring Foxes'
Kelly Louise Judd is an illustrator who lives in the mid-western United States.
She is inspired by flora, fauna and folklore, and has a deep appreciation of the
Arts and Crafts movement. Her illustrations have been featured in botanical and
children's books, and magazines, and on natural product labels. When she is not
working she can often be found outdoors tending her garden or simply staring at
plants. For more of her work visit www.kellylouisejudd.com

Design by Octavius Murray
Layout by Andrew Evans
Colophon and tailpiece by David Eccles

© The contributors 2020

Published by Slightly Foxed Limited
53 Hoxton Square
London N1 6PB

tel 020 7033 0258
email office@foxedquarterly.com
www.foxedquarterly.com

Slightly Foxed is published quarterly in early March, June, September and December

Annual subscription rates (4 issues)
UK and Ireland £48; Overseas £56

Single copies of this issue can be bought for £12.50 (UK) or £14.50 (Overseas)

All back issues in printed form are also available

ISBN 978-1-910898-39-0
ISSN 1742-5794

Printed and bound by Smith Settle, Yeadon, West Yorkshire

Contents

Contents

John Watson

The Slightly Foxed Podcast

A new episode of our podcast is available on the 15th of every month. To listen, visit www.foxedquarterly.com/pod or search for Slightly Foxed on Audioboom, iTunes or your podcast app.

Subscriber Benefits

Slightly Foxed can obtain any books reviewed in this issue, whether new or second-hand. To enquire about a book, to access the digital edition of *Slightly Foxed* or to view a list of membership benefits, visit www.foxedquarterly.com/members or contact the office: 020 7033 0258/office@foxedquarterly.com.

From the Editors

It's spring again, and a bit of news that feels cheering in today's disordered world reaches us via an unsolicited email from 'the world's leading market intelligence agency'. It seems that the number of Brits who bought a print book was up last year from 51 per cent in 2018 to 56 per cent. The main reason people gave was that they prefer physical books to reading on devices. E-books certainly have their uses, but there are very particular experiences attached to the reading of a physical book, particularly a second-hand one – its look, its feel, its smell, its history as evidenced by the clues left on it and in it by previous owners. Every physical book, like a person, tells a story of its own in a way no digital book can, however convenient.

We had a fascinating discussion on this subject with Chris Saunders, Managing Director of Henry Sotheran, the world's oldest antiquarian bookshop, in our October podcast (No. 12). For anyone who hasn't yet caught up with that episode, it's well worth a listen. And if you feel you would probably enjoy podcasts but don't quite know how to get started, do get in touch with Hattie, Jess or Anna on the office number to see if they can help.

This season's Slightly Foxed Edition takes us back to another disordered era in our history, that of the Second World War as experienced by a very unsnobbish and unconventional aristocrat, Hermione, Countess of Ranfurly. When her husband Dan was called up in 1939 and news came that he was permitted to take a servant with him – in this case their portly and characterful cook-butler Whitaker – but not his newly married wife, Hermione decided to defy regulations. With a Colt revolver hidden inside her girdle, she took ship to Egypt in search of her husband, vowing never to return until she and Dan were reunited. Likeable and capable, she was soon working for SOE in Cairo, and later as right-hand woman to General 'Jumbo' Wilson. The diary she kept during those years was eventually published as *To War with Whitaker* (see p.13). It's a sparkling, very human and often very funny behind-the-scenes account of the war and its personalities, and a touching love story.

This spring, to chime with the reissue of Rosemary Sutcliff's brilliant Roman novels in our Cubs series, we're bringing her own memoir, *Blue Remembered Hills*, back into print again in a Plain Foxed Edition. This was the very first book we published when we started the SFEs in 2008, and we've always felt a particular affection for it. It is the story of a child who grew up physically disabled by a severe form of juvenile arthritis, and who through will and imagination became a respected painter of miniatures and then a hugely successful children's author. It's a book full of the joy of living, a moving story of finding a vocation, which is as vivid and absorbing as any of Sutcliff's children's books.

Finally, on p.25 you'll find a piece by T. M. Delaney, the winner of the 2019 *SF* Writers' Competition – more evidence of the writing talent that we know lurks among our readers. And congratulations to Anthony Flack, the winner of our eleventh annual crossword competition, who receives a free annual subscription. For those of you still chewing your pencils, the answers are on p.96.

GAIL PIRKIS & HAZEL WOOD

Asking the Right Questions

DAVID GILMOUR

Aspiring young writers of fiction wish to be stylish. For many of them style is more essential than content, perhaps more important than sincerity. They want their prose to be inimitable, like Conrad's or Hemingway's, so that readers might identify their authorship from a single paragraph. As a young man, I was certainly like that, even though fiction didn't turn out to be my thing. And of course I preferred to read novels by writers who themselves had a pronounced style.

More than forty years ago, when reading Orwell's collected essays, I came across an autobiographical note that the author had written in 1940. After listing his favourite modern writers – Joyce, Eliot and D. H. Lawrence – he declared that the one who had influenced him most was Somerset Maugham, whom he admired immensely 'for his power of telling a story straightforwardly and without frills'. Despite my respect for Orwell's judgement, I was suspicious of that phrase about 'frills' – it suggested he was dismissing style – but I dutifully read some of Maugham's novels and stories.

What disillusionment I felt! How could Orwell have admired a writer who described people in such banal language, how one man was 'large and stoutish' while another was big 'but fat, with grey hair';

W. Somerset Maugham's Far Eastern short stories are available in three paperback volumes – *Far Eastern Tales*, *More Far Eastern Tales* and *The Narrow Corner* – as is *The Painted Veil* (1925), from Vintage at £9.99 each. Selina Hastings's masterly biography, *The Secret Lives of Somerset Maugham* (2009), is available in paperback from John Murray: 640pp • £16.99 • ISBN 9780719565557.

or a woman who was 'shortish and stout' and another who was 'tall-ish . . . with a good deal of pale brown hair'? How did an author help convey a scene in the Tropics with the phrase 'the sun beat fiercely' or tell us much about China with the clichéd and portentous state-ment, 'Here was the East, immemorial, dark and inscrutable.' When I later read Maugham's own assessment that he had 'no lyrical qual-ity', 'little gift of metaphor' and 'small power of imagination', I felt that at least he possessed some self-awareness.

Some decades later I stayed a few days in Singapore. I was travel-ling from Perth, Scotland to Perth, Australia (rather a long way to go to watch England lose a Test Match) and thought I should acknow-ledge the fact that Asia lay in between by stopping off somewhere. Like many of us, I enjoy reading writers in appropriate places – Ruskin in Venice, Proust in Normandy – so I tried Maugham again. Of course nowadays Singapore is no more redolent of Maugham than it is of Raffles; looking for footsteps there is as futile as trying to listen to a nightingale on Hampstead Heath. Yet this time I did appreciate the fourth point of Maugham's self-assessment: that he possessed 'an acute power of observation' and that he was able to see 'a great many things that other people missed'. His characters might be banal and be described banally, but they were at least real and living in real situations. I recognized that Maugham possessed extra-ordinary psychological insight.

Last winter in India I reread the Far East fiction, the short stories and two novels, *The Painted Veil* and *The Narrow Corner*. (I did not go back to *The Moon and Sixpence*, which is partly set in Polynesia – too far east – and libels Gauguin's character, unappealing though it may have been.) I had several days to spare between the Arts Festival in Goa and *The Times of India* Litfest in Mumbai, and I spent them beside a bay in western India. Luckily there were no tourists there because some years ago an environmental disaster (some blamed the tsunami, others the grounding of a vast tanker) had caused nearly all the sand to disappear.

Somerset Maugham by
Graham Sutherland © NPG

Each afternoon I read Maugham under a rough canopy on the beach, watching fishermen bringing in the catch, listening to the sounds of women shouting to each other in Konkani, their voices competing with the screeching of parrots and the cawing of crows. The bay was congested with fishing boats, blue hulls under green awnings, lying low in the water. In the evening a black bullock with painted yellow horns was led along the beach, and I watched the sun going down beyond the headland, silhouetting the palm trees against the sky. As I sat enjoying the books, I felt that it was a setting Maugham would have appreciated, and I wondered why he had never written a story set in India. Later I discovered it was because, 'so far as [Indian] stories were concerned', he believed that 'Kipling had written all the good ones' – an absurd belief, as Maugham himself came to realize. Kipling had lived in a couple of cities in northern India and had returned to England at the age of 23. He had left plenty of scope and space for a rival storyteller.

Maugham's travels in eastern Asia took in Burma, Siam, China and Cambodia, but the best of his stories are located in and around the Federated Malay States. He actually visited the Far East only twice, in 1921 and 1925, spending a total of ten months there, a far shorter period than Orwell's five years as a policeman in Burma or Kipling's six and a half years as a journalist in India.[*] This accounts for certain limitations in his work. Unlike Orwell he made no attempt to write about imperialism and its effects on the people under colonial rule. And unlike Kipling he made little effort to make

---

[*] Both Orwell and Kipling were born in India, the first in Bengal, where he remained for a year, the second in Bombay, where he stayed until he was 5.

real characters of his 'natives': there is no Lama or Babu or dowager Sahiba as in *Kim*, but a few rather stock characters: the houseboy, the discarded mistress, the wily Chinese clerk in Singapore.

Yet as a portrait of the British in the Far East at the time, the stories are extraordinarily perceptive. They contain a surprising amount of tension and passion; there are an unusual number of murders as a result; and there is enough adultery to rival Kipling's *Under the Deodars* and *Plain Tales from the Hills*. Yet behind the excitements Maugham's descriptions of the realities of colonial life are concise and well-observed. And as I read them under the awning on my sandless beach, I recognized that they exhibited the three virtues he regarded as essential: lucidity, simplicity and euphony.

In her wonderful biography *The Secret Lives of Somerset Maugham*, Selina Hastings ascribed the success of *The Painted Veil* (which is set in China) to the author's 'two greatest strengths, his dramatist's infallible ear for dialogue and his instinct for psychological truth'. The Malayan tales contain additional strengths such as a vivid sense of place and an understanding of the lives of the British expatriates, the planters and the district officers, the routines of social life, the drive to the club, the evening cocktail and the bridge table afterwards. Maugham was well attuned to the nuances of social class, and he could sense both the superior attitudes of officials and the resentments of the men who ran the rubber plantations. And he observed the monotony of expatriate life and its loneliness, not just the boredom of wives with nothing to do but boss the servants, but also their vulnerability, their sense of alienness, their reliance on routine to keep themselves from losing control and 'going to seed'.

Maugham is both compassionate and empathetic to such people. In 'The Outstation' he does not mock the rather absurd figure of Mr Warburton, a senior official who dresses as if for a club in Pall Mall even when he is dining alone in the jungle. And he is sympathetic to lonely wives even when they are adulterous. His bisexuality (a good deal more inclined towards men than to women) may have wrecked his marriage, but it helped provide him with a sensibility seldom rivalled among male novelists in his handling of female behaviour and motivation. He was thus able to inhabit his women characters as Alberto Moravia did in his remarkable novel about an Italian prostitute, *La romana*. Kitty Fane in *The Painted Veil*, torn between a despised husband and a caddish lover (with an appalling mother in the background), is one of the great female figures of fiction.

Somerset Maugham's 'research' technique was simple: he travelled, he observed and he listened. His travelling companion or 'secretary', Gerald Haxton, got drunk and behaved badly but he did meet people in bars who told him good stories which he repeated to his employer. And Maugham himself was capable of acquiring 'copy' simply by asking the right questions. In his story 'Masterson' he described how a man 'in some lonely post in the jungle' would give him a drink and then – after a few more drinks – say 'Would it bore you awfully if I told you about' such-and-such an incident? In his memoir *The Summing Up* he recorded how, when 'sitting over a siphon or two and a bottle of whisky . . . [within] the radius of an acetylene lamp . . . a man has told me stories about himself that I was sure he had never told to a living soul'.

His temporary confidants may have enjoyed Maugham's companionship for an evening, but they were not so appreciative when they read their stories, only mildly disguised, some years later in magazines and books. As one civil servant observed, Maugham's passage through the Federated Malay States was 'clearly marked by a trail of angry people' who accused him of betraying their confidences and writing about only 'the worst and least representative aspects of European life' there: 'murder, cowardice, drink, seduction, adultery'. Similar accusations (minus the murders) were made of Kipling's tales of Simla.

Yet there was a difference. The characters and events of Kipling's stories were very seldom recognizable; Maugham's often were. When drunk in a bar, Haxton learned about the murderous couple who became the Cartwrights in 'Footsteps in the Jungle'. Staying in Kuala Lumpur, Maugham heard from her lawyer about Ethel Proudlock, a woman who in 1911 had murdered her lover after she discovered he had a Chinese mistress. The crime of Mrs Proudlock (transformed into Mrs Crosbie) was retold in the story 'The Letter' and publicized in *Hearst's International* in 1924, in Maugham's collection *The Casuarina Tree* in 1926, in the theatre (the murderess played by Gladys Cooper) in 1927 and in a Warner Brothers film (the role played by Bette Davis) in 1940.

Perhaps we may sympathize with both sides, the artist who immortalized a British society living a brief, exotic existence in a part of the globe as far from Britain as it is possible to be, and a group of vulnerable men and women that had welcomed a visitor who, after enjoying their hospitality, broadcast their defects in three different art forms. Whatever the wrongs of the matter, it says something for Maugham's talent that, however banally Mrs Crosbie is described physically – 'graceful' and 'unassuming' with 'a great deal of light brown hair' – she was a character sufficiently interesting to be played by two great actresses.

DAVID GILMOUR is the author of *Curzon, The Long Recessional: The Imperial Life of Rudyard Kipling* and *The British in India*, all of which were reissued in paperback by Penguin last year.

Love, War and the Countess

PETER J. CONRADI

I think it was my old friend the *Evening Standard* columnist Angus McGill who recommended Hermione, Countess of Ranfurly's war diaries: Angus would have loved her unpretentious skill at conjuring up another place, another time. Published in 1994 under the title *To War with Whitaker*, they have the enthralling quality that Dostoevsky called 'living life', offering you a front-row seat at the great unfolding historical drama of the Second World War. They were written on the hoof, in moments snatched at the end of long, exhausting working days when letter-writing had also to be fitted in. Fifty years later she prepared them for publication and was astonished by their success.

'In three phrases, she paints a man, in two more, she gives the background and then . . . she sets them in motion, they talk, gesticulate and move about . . . I could have listened to her forever.' Thus Hermione praises the descriptive powers of a Beirut acquaintance. She could equally have been describing her own unshowy gift for bringing her world to life.

Dan and Hermione Ranfurly were on a deer-stalking holiday in Scotland when war was declared. They had met and fallen in love in Australia in 1937 when he was aide-de-camp to Lord Gowrie, the Governor-General, and she was personal assistant to Lord Wakehurst, Governor of New South Wales, and they had married in January 1939 when both were 25. On hearing the news of war they returned to London, where a telegram from Dan's Yeomanry regiment told him to report for duty. Dan turned to their portly cook-butler Whitaker and asked if he was coming too.

'The old fatty looked over the top of his spectacles and said "To the war, my Lord? Very good, my Lord." Then we started to pack.'

If this suggests an *Upstairs, Downstairs* scenario it is misleading. Whitaker is as much friend as servant and when, long after the war, he dies, as Hermione describes in a memoir she wrote in her old age, she and Dan cried 'like children'. From a desperately poor north of England family, a piano-player, resourceful, talented and self-educated, and so fat that the cinema seat breaks under his weight when he is watching Olivier's *Henry V*, Whitaker shadows Hermione through much of the war, providing comic relief.

The real joke, however, was that a Yeomanry officer was permitted to take his servant to war but not his wife. 'Grannies, sisters, mothers, mistresses and regular Army wives may go – only Yeomanry wives will not be allowed to go overseas.' Dan and Hermione joke that they might have to get divorced in order to stay together. It is satisfying to watch Hermione outmanoeuvre these absurd regulations. Soon after Dan leaves for Palestine she acquires visas from a shady travel agent to cross France and sail from Marseilles to Egypt to be reunited with him. She travels with a newly purchased .25 Colt revolver hidden – though she can't yet shoot – inside her elastic girdle.

There was a desperate shortage of English-speaking secretaries in the Middle East, and Hermione, though well-connected – her aunt was lady-in-waiting to Queen Mary – was also impoverished and had trained as a shorthand typist, working for the War Office. Nonetheless a fanatical one-eyed Brigadier, bent on forcibly evacuating illegal war wives, sneers, 'You can't expect me to believe that a Countess can type.' Soldiers duly take her away and Dan receives a £40 bill for her evacuation to South Africa. In Cape Town she quietly jumps ship, asking a taxi-driver to drive her the 6,000-odd miles back to Cairo. Though unsuccessful she was lucky. The ship she had just left was sunk off the coast of Ireland and among the casualties was her best friend 'Toby' Wallace, who had followed her husband to Palestine, but was now returning home.

A Cape Town banker loans Hermione £115 to pay for a three-day

'We went riding after learning that, like all Yeomanry wives, I would not
be allowed to go overseas.'

flying-boat trip back to Cairo, where, by December 1940, she has
found a job as confidential secretary to the head of the Special
Operations Executive, responsible for dropping agents behind enemy
lines to help organize local resistance. It is fascinating to see her move
swiftly from being *persona non grata* to being at the very centre of
operations. SOE activities were both maverick – flouting directives
from London – and also duplicitous, covering this up. Security was
lax and SOE wasted 'fabulous' sums of money with dubious results.
Hermione decides to leak this information to Anthony Eden, then
Foreign Secretary, secreting sensitive documents in her bra when
leaving the office at night and making copies at home before returning the originals the following morning. A reform of SOE results and
she starts to be seen as a formidable asset.

In April 1941, Dan goes missing. Four agonizing weeks later she
learns via the Red Cross that he is still alive. His first letter as a POW
in Italy takes five months to reach her. She puts on a brave face by
day and unleashes her misery only when closing her bedroom door
at night; the smell of Dan's hairbrushes makes her cry. This new sep-
aration lasts three years: they were finally reunited in May 1944, after
he had spent ten dangerous months on the run in northern Italy.

In July 1941 she moves to work in Jerusalem as personal assistant to the High Commissioner in Palestine where her efficiency, discretion and social skills evidently tell. By October 1942 General Wavell is offering a posting within his HQ in India (Hermione noting Lady Wavell's 'delightfully vague air, as if she had lost or forgotten something') and Freya Stark wants her as an assistant; but she chooses to work as private secretary to General Jumbo Wilson (later Supreme Allied Commander in the Mediterranean). He has a 'twinkle in his eyes [and] is so large he looks silly holding a cup and saucer. He puffs

Whitaker in Bethlehem, 1940

when he sits down and he puffs when he gets up again.' Hermione clearly becomes indispensable to the General, and only his wife's jealousy eventually saves her from having to accompany him to America at the end of the war.

Soon her job is to be sent anywhere at any time, meeting aeroplanes, playing hostess on official occasions – at one point she helps organize a lunch party for 86 guests – comforting lonely officers, giving tea to Partisan dictators. Americans, French, Greeks, Poles, Czechs and Egyptians pass through her office

and she has to remember all their names. She has the fun of being 'in the know', reading Churchill's cables to General Jumbo, knowing about D-Day in advance, watching the great come and go. At one point she helps a 20-year-old royalist Greek, who would otherwise almost certainly have been killed, to escape by borrowing a uniform for him. But there is also much carbon paper and a lot of bores. When she visits the sick and wounded, their lack of self-pity moves her. She determinedly suppresses her tears and any reference to activities to which the lame or sightless can no longer look forward.

'In a war', she writes, 'animals and birds help one very much.' A white mouse with pink eyes called Fuad, slipped into her pocket by a Cairo shopkeeper, consoles her and quickly becomes a general pet.

And she loves birds – taking a budgerigar to Egypt in 1940, and a parrot home in 1944. She values those many who make her laugh, from King Farouk to Lord Beaverbrook. She is friendly, brave, un-snobbish, full of sharp little observations that bring people alive. In Jerusalem she makes friends with Freya Stark, 'very small and ugly. She wears eccentric clothes and has her hair looped down on one side to hide something. It is said she fell on to, or in front of a mowing machine when she was young and lost an ear . . .'

Hermione Ranfurly would surely have laughed at any suggestion that her book was 'Tolstoyan'. Yet she conveys what it feels like for the lonely individual to be caught up in a vast cataclysm. She was evidently a sympathetic listener in whom many confided, and there are few major players in the theatre of war whom she does not at some point meet. Tito, short, stocky and dressed to kill, talks bad German with her, Nancy Mitford's lover and de Gaulle's future *chef de cabinet* Gaston Palewski chats her up, true to form.

She is tolerant of difficult, egotistical men. Orde Wingate wants her to parachute into the Horn of Africa to provide secretarial assis-tance while he raises a revolt in Abyssinia; General Patton, who insults both a GI and a distinguished professor who is showing him the sights, she finds 'very direct and great fun'; Randolph Churchill and Evelyn Waugh shout at each other like furious schoolboys and argue about nothing, but she is 'very fond of Randolph' for all his nuisance value and rudeness. Though she has sharp comments to make, she nonetheless likes almost everyone, with the exception of the British general Montgomery. 'Of all the VIPs we look after, he is the least attractive.' Many of her friends have more sympathy for his German opponent, General Rommel.

She also has an unfailing ability to find the right person to help her at the right time. Home in London in January 1945 she bumps into one-eyed General Carton de Wiart, believed to have been a model for the bloodthirsty Brigadier Ritchie Hook in Waugh's *Sword of Honour* trilogy. Hermione learns that the General, who is about to fly to China, owns his own plane. So she hitches a lift from him to 'anywhere in the Mediterranean' to be near Dan once more.

She never doubts that war is an abomination. Midway through watching film of the 'liberation' of Belsen she has to leave the cinema: 'beyond our wildest dreams of atrocity . . . How can anyone ever forgive the Germans?' The annihilation of Hiroshima and Nagasaki appals and terrifies her. Half the Ranfurlys' generation of friends, 'so young and attractive and so brave', are dead, others wounded, six years of their youth stolen. By 1944 she fears that there is little hope for humanity. Yet that war also brings out the best as well as the worst is a platitude that she brings memorably to life. War is unspeakable, but – as commentators since Homer have observed – it also enables singular acts of heroism and kindness.

PETER J. CONRADI has written – *inter alia* – biographies of Iris Murdoch and Frank Thompson, *Going Buddhist* and *At the Bright Hem of God*. Writing a family memoir has made him think afresh about the Second World War – his father escaped from Normandy ten days after Dunkirk and married a week later.

Hermione, Countess of Ranfurly's *To War with Whitaker* (416pp), is now available in a limited and numbered cloth-bound edition of 2,000 copies (subscribers: UK & Eire £17, Overseas £19; non-subscribers: UK & Eire £18.50, Overseas £20.50). All prices include post and packing. Copies may be ordered by post (53 Hoxton Square, London N1 6PB), by phone (020 7033 0258) or via our website www.foxedquarterly.com.

Streets, Streets, Streets

FELICITY JAMES

I'm deep in mountain territory, with a pot noodle and a stack of Post-its in front of me. It's past midnight, and my final undergraduate exams are just around the corner. Feverishly, between forkfuls, I'm wandering on high over hill and vale; I'm crossing the Alps; I'm brooding on the Wordsworthian sublime. Every so often, I'll note down an Important Thought on my pink Post-its. Nature! Morality! Mountains!

The Prelude is open in front of me, Wordsworth's epic poem of natural inspiration, nourished by the Lakeland landscape of his childhood:

> Ye Presences of Nature, in the sky
> And on the earth! Ye Visions of the hills!

Alongside this, I'm reading Coleridge's unsurpassed conversation poem 'This Lime-Tree Bower my Prison', addressed to his friend Charles Lamb, 'of the India House, London'. Here the poet must rest at home, debarred by injury from accompanying his friends on a country walk. Those friends were William and Dorothy Wordsworth,

---

There have been two editions of the Lambs' letters: *The Letters of Charles and Mary Anne Lamb*, ed. Edwin W. Marrs, Jr., 3 vols. [which go up to 1817], Cornell University Press, 1975, and *The Letters of Charles and Mary Lamb*, ed. E. V. Lucas, 3 vols., Dent, 1935. Sadly neither is still in print.

The band of devotees in the Charles Lamb Society, who celebrate his birthday each year with a lunch, would always be glad to hear from new readers of the Lambs: see www.charleslambsociety.com.

and Charles Lamb, on a rare, brief visit from London. Lamb is depicted as 'my gentle-hearted Charles', 'who has pined and hunger'd after Nature, many a year,/ In the great City pent,' but who is now released to enjoy the true delights of the countryside.

Confined to the lime-tree bower, the poet enviously imagines the pleasures they are experiencing in the 'wide landscape'. But gradually he comes to the realization that nature may be appreciated even in the smallest of spaces, focusing on the sun-dappled detail of a leaf and the 'solitary humble-bee' in the nearby bean flowers. And he hopes that Lamb, too, who has struggled with 'evil, and pain/And strange calamity', may find a healing power in nature.

My eye drifts down to the footnote, which gives some details of the 'strange calamity' that had befallen Charles Lamb the year before: the death of his mother at the hands of his sister, Mary, in a fit of mania. Charles, just 21 at the time, undertook to look after Mary himself, saving her from consignment to Bedlam. Apart from some brief spells she had to spend in asylums, the two lived together in a sort of 'double singleness' until Charles's death in 1834.

This is what lies behind Coleridge's evocation of his 'gentle-hearted' friend, and his hope that Charles will find 'deep joy' in nature. But it's with a slight shock that I see what Lamb actually thought about his beautiful portrayal in this poem. 'For God's sake (I never was more serious),' he told Coleridge in August 1800, 'don't make me ridiculous any more by terming me gentle-hearted in print.' A week or so later, in case Coleridge hadn't got the message, he returned to the complaint: 'Please to blot out gentle hearted, and substitute drunken dog, ragged head, seld-shaven, odd-ey'd, stuttering, or any other epithet which truly and properly belongs to the Gentleman in question'.[*] Steeped in Romantic transcendence, this strikes me with the thrill of blasphemy. I'm hooked.

---

[*] Lamb had one blue and one brown eye. He was also a stutterer, slightly unkempt and given to over-indulge in rum and water, and 'egg-hot'.

Charles Lamb is better known – if known at all these days – as an essayist, and his marvellously eclectic, evasive *Essays of Elia* featured in the last issue of *Slightly Foxed* (no. 64). With Mary, he collaborated on some of the best-loved children's books of the nineteenth century, their prose adaptations *Tales from Shakespeare*, and the poignant stories of *Mrs Leicester's School*. But it's as letter-writers that they truly excel. When I tracked down a copy of the letters of Charles and Mary Lamb, I discovered that this habit of answering back, of wry, sly, disputation with the greats, was no one-off.

Take Lamb's letter to his friend the mathematics tutor and sinologist Thomas Manning in November 1800. He is sorry to tell Manning that he won't be able to come to see him in Cambridge after all, since there is a chance of visiting the Lake District. And who would turn down the chance actually to *see* Wordsworth and Coleridge amid the mountains?

> I need not describe to you the expectations which such an one as myself, pent up all my life in a dirty city, have formed of a tour to the *Lakes*. Consider, Grasmere! Ambleside! Wordsworth! Coleridge! I hope you will.

There follows a contemplative pause, a blank space. Manning must meekly accept his demotion.

But when he, and the reader of Lamb's letters, turns the page, we find a bold statement:

> Hills, woods, Lakes and mountains, to the Eternal Devil. I will eat snipes with thee, Thomas Manning. Only confess, confess a *Bite*.

A bite, in eighteenth-century terms, could mean a hoax or fraud – and Lamb's letters take great delight in hoaxing, joking, trickery. But the 'bite' is also a peculiarly appropriate term for Lamb's letters, because they are distinguished by their witty, cutting edge, made the sharper because he is such a good reader, and devoted friend, of the poets he criticizes. Here he knowingly takes the phrase from the Coleridge poem, 'in City pent', and turns it around. Forget nature: he can find joy and healing in London itself. For Lamb, it is not a 'dirty city', but a place (like Coleridge's lime-tree bower) where each tiny detail can bring inspiration and pleasure:

> Streets, streets, streets, markets, theatres, churches, Covent Gardens, Shops sparkling with pretty faces of industrious milliners, neat sempstresses, Ladies cheapening, Gentlemen behind counters lying, Authors in the street with spectacles . . . Lamps lit at night, Pastry-cook & Silver smith shops, Beautiful Quakers of Pentonville, noise of coaches, drousy cry of mechanic watchmen at night, with Bucks reeling home drunk if you happen to wake at midnight, cries of fire & stop thief; Inns of court (with their learned air, and halls, and Butteries, just like Cambridge colleges), old Book stalls, Jeremy Taylors, Burtons on melancholy, and Religio Medici's on every stall – . These are thy Pleasures O London with-the-many-sins –

Those three opening beats – 'Streets, streets, streets' – act as an incantation, summoning the tumbling, breathless hurry of London life to the page. Things and places and noises crowd into the same sentence with amoral urban haste. Instead of the steady, timeless 'presences of Nature' made sacred in the poetry of Wordsworth and Coleridge, we encounter bargaining ladies, lying salesmen, drunks, thieves, whores. This is no random assortment of city objects but is carefully structured around allusions to Lamb's own life – his unrequited affection for a young beautiful Quaker lady, his birthplace in the Inner Temple, his love of Jeremy Taylor and Robert Burton's seventeenth-century texts.

Just as Wordsworth's poetry shows how important the scenes of childhood are to shaping later life, so too does Lamb emphasize the power of his own local affections, his favourite homely things:

– old chairs, old tables, streets, squares, where I have sunned myself, my old school, – these are my mistresses, have I not enough, without your mountains? –

This comes from a letter to Wordsworth, of all people, where Lamb thanks him for a copy of *Lyrical Ballads*, and an invitation to visit, but tells him, 'I don't much care if I never see a mountain in my life' (30 January 1801). Instead, he gently offers a city-based appreciation of his friend's poetry – part defiance, part homage.

The Lake poets did not take the criticism well. As Lamb tells Manning in subsequent letters, both Wordsworth and Coleridge immediately sent long letters of 'four sweating pages' apiece rebuking him and assuring him, 'when the works of a man of true Genius, such as W. undoubtedly was, do not please me at first sight, I should suspect the fault to lie "in me & not in them" – &c. &c. &c. &c. &c. . . .' That clutter of etceteras tells us all we need to know about Wordsworth and Coleridge's high-handed style, but Lamb was unabashed, commenting to Manning that 'my *Arse tickles red* from the northern castigation'.

In spite of this ticklish irreverence, the letters are also testaments of friendship, running from the 1790s to the 1830s. Nothing, deep down, could shake the affection between Charles and Mary and old friends such as William and Dorothy Wordsworth, Coleridge or William Hazlitt. Charles worked tirelessly to get information and consolation from his India House connections when the Wordsworths' brother John went down off the Dorset coast with the East India vessel he commanded. 'You have not mourned without one to have a feeling of it,' he wrote to the Wordsworths (4 March 1805). Alongside his letters mourning John come words from Mary, who reassures Dorothy that her memories of her lost brother will eventually become 'a real & everlasting source of comfort to you', a truth drawn from 'my own experience in sorrow' (7 May 1805). This, perhaps, is what gives the letters of the Lambs a lasting power: that shared experience in sorrow, and the knowledge of grief and pain and strange calamity which deepens and darkens their writing.

Charles's letters far outnumber Mary's, but her voice is everywhere in his prose, sometimes quoted, sometimes in the shape of postscripts or comments. Her letters to her friend Sarah Stoddart (later Hazlitt's wife) are gems, 'journal-like letters, of the daily what-we-do-matters', brimming with gossip and affection. She shows herself as keen a reader of the London scene as Charles, evoking the city life she and Sarah had enjoyed together from a slightly different angle, 'bustling down Fleet-Market-in-all-its-glory of a saturday night, admiring the stale peas and co'lly flowers and cheap'ning small bits of mutton and veal for our sunday's dinner's' (1 December 1802).

You'll have to engage in your own bargaining, though, to find an edition of the letters. Other Romantic writers have lavish sets of published correspondence and annotated works, but the Lambs have been poorly served by posterity. A new edition of their work is under way, but for the moment even to find a complete set of the letters is a difficult task. Hunt out the E. V. Lucas editions of the 1930s, if you can. Edwin Marrs's fine scholarly edition undertaken in the 1970s was left uncompleted at his death, but it scrupulously attempts to render the Lambs' enthusiastic hands, veering into huge capitals or breaking off to doodle. There are plenty of Victorian volumes of selections of the Lambs' letters, though, and burrowing into second-hand stock is a particularly appropriate way to remember these authors, with their love of 'Old Book stalls' and battered copies. And you'll have the deep satisfaction of having tracked down the hidden byways of Romantic writing: not sublime mountain visions, but side-streets, smoky rooms and friendly, rum-flavoured conversations.

FELICITY JAMES has spent two decades in the company of Charles and Mary Lamb, and is now editing their work for children. As one of the chairs of the Charles Lamb Society, she is the proud current possessor of an actual chair said to have belonged to Charles Lamb – in which this piece was written.

How to Cook a Fox

T. M. DELANEY

URING a time when I was unable to work I read a lot, and randomly, picking up whatever took my fancy in the local bookshop. I had recently moved to an old farmstead on Orkney with enough space to grow some vegetables and berry fruit – not exactly living off the land, but an exciting departure for someone who had always lived in a town. One day I chanced upon Patience Gray's *Honey from a Weed*, took it home and soon found myself fantasizing about planting olive trees – although to tell the truth I always knew that olives would never thrive in a latitude so high that it is impossible to grow wheat here.

Subtitled 'Fasting and Feasting in Tuscany, Catalonia, the Cyclades and Apulia', *Honey from a Weed* (1986) is based on the proposition that what is best in human culture has been created and refined by necessity. In the early 1960s Gray set off for the Mediterranean with the sculptor Norman Mommens to search for marble around the Mediterranean which, she writes, 'precipitated us out of modern life into the company of marble artisans and wine-growers in Carrara and into an isolated community of "Bronze Age" farmers on Naxos'. There she found food cultures rooted in a cycle of feast and famine conditioned by the seasons, where a multitude of delicious dishes were conjured from sparse ingredients. 'Good cooking', Gray says, 'is the result of a balance struck between frugality and liberality.'

Both Gray and Mommens had abandoned orthodox careers in

Patience Gray, *Honey from a Weed* (1986)
Prospect · Pb · 375pp · £20 · ISBN 9781903018200

England to pursue this vagabond life, Gray as women's page editor of the *Observer*, and Mommens as an artist and art school teacher. Eventually they settled in a farmhouse in Puglia called Spigolizzi. Here, with neither electricity nor running water, they led a deliberately 'simple' life, growing olives and making their own wine.

To call *Honey from a Weed* a cookbook would be a bit like calling *Moby Dick* a book about fishing. As a cookbook it serves well enough, full of usable recipes culled from the cuisines of the places where Gray lived. But it is much, much more than that: it is a discourse on Mediterranean culture and the lives of the rural poor, a herbal, a work of social anthropology, a biographical narrative and a paean to a way of life that, if not completely dead, was already fatally wounded. It's full of stories about the people Gray met, memorable characters shaped by the rigours of peasant life for the most part, but also artist friends, gastronomes and book collectors. It is often very funny.

It is also a work of immense erudition: a passage on the origins of marzipan refers back to the fourth-century Greek poet and gastronome Archistratus and to an Italian cookbook of 1570; Horace features in an examination of the origins of pasta; and there is a learned discussion on the tendency of beans to provoke flatulence. It also has the best bibliography of all the books I own, to the extent that I sometimes take it down simply for the pleasure of looking through it. What other book on food has a bibliography that includes Alfred Jarry's *Ubu Roi*? Or *Tristram Shandy*? Or Malatesta's *L'anarquía*? Or Aeschylus or Hesiod or Eric Partridge's *Shakespeare's Bawdy*? It is so diverse that it could really form the basis for a course in European culture.

I must confess I was puzzled at first by the extent to which Gray promotes the eating of what she insists on calling 'weeds', but it wasn't long before I began to see the ragged dandelion in a new light. The peasants among whom Gray lived foraged for a large part of their diet and she had to learn, little by little, what local wild plants could be used in everyday dishes. One of her instructors was a child:

> At La Barozza I had a profitable weed lesson from a little girl of seven called Eugenia, who had an amazing weed vocabulary culled from the vineyard that her father worked. As she picked each plant, she said 'This is for cooking' or 'This is for salad' (her plant categories).

Radicchio, dandelions, comfrey, sorrel, wild fennel, wild beets, fat hen, samphire and saltwort, elderflower, broom rape, wild asparagus, tassel hyacinth, purslane, angelica and field poppy are all discussed, and as I write this with the book beside me, it has fallen open at a chapter entitled 'Fungi and Michelangelo'. Gray also provides recipes for several species of snail.

Nowadays foraged food appears on the menus of expensive restaurants, which might have seemed paradoxical to Gray (although she would surely have approved). She would certainly have been in sympathy with the movement to eat less meat. When she wrote, a new prosperity was changing the custom of generations in the communities where she lived: whereas meat had formerly been restricted to Sundays and feast days, buying meat on any day was becoming an ostentatious way of showing the world that one was prospering. 'I am not alone in my conviction that one should eat less meat,' she wrote.

Yet I can't imagine that she would ever have been in sympathy with either veganism or vegetarianism. Some of the most memorable passages in *Honey from a Weed* describe the eating of items from which most of us in this pasteurized and shrink-wrapped age would recoil. In Naxos she is offered and eats (albeit with a certain amount of reluctance) the grilled head of a small bird and the fried spleen of a goat. Among many recipes is one for cooking a fox, 'given to me by an old anarchist in Carrara'. It employs the *alla cacciatora* method which, she tells us, can also be used for badger.

Gray defines eccentricity as 'living according to priorities established by one's own experience' and she is always alive to what is singular in the people around her. In *Honey from a Weed* she celebrates their resilience and their independent spirit, epitomized most purely, perhaps, by the marble workers of Carrara, but also encountered in fishermen, peasants, sculptors and booksellers (who she sees as 'legendary figures' in their search for authenticity in the written word). One chapter is a homage to a wheeler-dealer she meets in Puglia, 'an old fox, a dark horse, a crocodile', an expert in the art of greasing the right hands, a teller of tales of his own cunning, who keeps an excellent table.

As for me, the cultivation of olives in the windy north was never anything but a fantasy, but these days I grow a few potatoes and some tomatoes in a greenhouse, and on fine days I venture out to try and improve my plant identification skills. I have no illusions about becoming self-sufficient, but I am working my way through the books in Gray's bibliography and her writing is still an inspiration.

T. M. DELANEY has been a teacher and a council officer. He now lives in the teeth of a gale in a house overlooking Scapa Flow. His article won the 2019 *Slightly Foxed* Writers' Competition.

Coming Home

ANN KENNEDY SMITH

We first meet the eponymous heroine of Brian Moore's novel *The Lonely Passion of Judith Hearne* (1955) shortly after she has moved into her new lodgings. As she carefully unpacks a silver-framed photograph of her Aunt D'Arcy and a religious image of the Sacred Heart, we sense her misgivings about 'the condition of the bed-springs, the shabbiness of the furniture and the run-down part of Belfast in which the room was situated'.

Judith Hearne is an unmarried, middle-aged woman living on precarious means in the 1950s. Both Miss Hearne (as she is always known) and the boarding-house have seen better days, but she does not dwell on her reduced circumstances for long. She takes pride in her neat appearance, devout Roman Catholicism and grammar-school education. The sparse furniture in her rented room can be moved to hide the stains, and her two pictures are comforting talismans: 'When they're with me, watching over me, a new place becomes home.'

Belfast is the setting for this modern classic about self-delusion, spiritual crisis and an awakening to a new truth. *The Lonely Passion of Judith Hearne* made its author famous and put the city on the world literary map. For the latter part of the twentieth century, however, Northern Ireland was a place associated with bitter conflict, not bleak social comedy. I was fortunate enough to grow up in a peaceful seaside town there, but when I first read Moore's novel in the 1980s, Belfast had long been ravaged by the Troubles. Perhaps it was because

Brian Moore, *The Lonely Passion of Judith Hearne* (1955)
Harper Perennial · Pb · 256pp · £8.99 · ISBN 9780007255610

of this that Bruce Beresford's 1987 film of the book relocated the story to Dublin. Maggie Smith and Bob Hoskins are excellent actors, but the book's essential Northern Irish geography is missing.

Brian Moore was born in 1921 and grew up in Clifton Street, then an affluent part of Belfast close to busy Royal Avenue. His father was a prominent surgeon and the first Catholic to be appointed to the Senate of Queen's University; his mother Eileen was a nurse from Donegal, twenty years younger than her husband. Dr James Moore's surgery was on the ground floor of their tall Victorian house, while Brian (always pronounced 'Bree-an' in the Gaelic way by his family) and his eight siblings spent their days in the spacious rooms above with their mother, nursemaid Nellie and two maiden aunts. Moore later described it as a 'house of women'. Just opposite was the Central Orange Hall with a statue of a conquering King William III on horseback on the roof, a constant reminder of the social and religious divisions of the city.

'Belfast and my childhood have made me suspicious of faiths, allegiances, certainties,' Moore wrote. 'It is time to leave home.' Aged 22, having failed at university and abandoned his Catholicism, he knew that to become a writer he would have to leave Ireland, just as his literary hero James Joyce had done before him. The Second World War gave him the opportunity. In 1943, as German bombs rained down on Belfast, he joined the British Army and served as an administrator on the edge of war zones in North Africa, Italy and France.

After the war, he worked for the United Nations in Warsaw. This international experience introduced him, as his biographer Denis Sampson observes, 'to a world without national or ethnic borders' and made a lasting impact on his imagination. In his later novels he often returned to those places that he called his 'emotional territories', and explored his fictional characters' inner conflicts in times and places as far apart as seventeenth-century Canada in *Black Robe* (1985), 1940s eastern Europe in *The Colour of Blood* (1987) and modern-day Haiti in *No Other Life* (1993).

In 1947 Moore settled in Montreal, where he found a job as a journalist and wrote a series of bestselling thrillers under pseudonyms. He married Jackie, a French-Canadian fellow journalist, and just before their son Michael was born in 1953, he became a Canadian citizen. By then, he was already at work on his first serious novel, one in which he would return to Belfast to 'write it out of my system', he thought. Only later did he realize that as well as setting out the bitter reasons why he had left Ireland, his novel touched on his own loneliness as an exile.

It was thanks to Diana Athill that *Judith Hearne*, as it was originally called, was published in London in 1955 (ten American publishers turned it down). As co-director of André Deutsch, she passionately championed Moore's book when others doubted, and in her memoir *Stet* she recalls meeting its author: 'a small, fat, round-headed, sharp-nosed man resembling a robin, whose flat Ulster accent was the first of its kind I had heard'. They became good friends and remained so until 1967 when, in the wake of a bitter divorce, Brian Moore abruptly ended their personal and professional relationship. Deutsch had published Moore's first five novels, including *The Luck of Ginger Coffey* (1960) and *The Emperor of Ice Cream* (1965). Others that he wrote later are 'outstandingly good', Athill writes, 'but to my mind he never wrote anything more moving and more true than *Judith Hearne*'.

It's a book that takes you into the heart of a claustrophobic post-war Belfast, a city where – in this novel at least – it never seems to stop raining.

> The rain began to patter again on the windows, growing heavier, soft persistent Irish rain coming up Belfast Lough, caught in the shadow of Cave Hill. It settled on the city, a night blanket of wetness.

Judith Hearne is all too familiar with the city's rain-sodden streets and chilly bedsits, moving as she does from one sordid lodging to another. Now in her forties, she has spent most of her adult life looking after her 'dear aunt', who selfishly made sure that her niece never married or went to secretarial college. Her aunt's death has left her vulnerable and alone, eking out a meagre living as a piano teacher. Her religiousness takes the form of observance rather than faith, and she snobbishly refuses to mix with lower-class Catholics. Her Sunday afternoon tea with the O'Neills, a university professor and his family, is the only bright point of Miss Hearne's week, but certainly not of theirs. The O'Neills' comfortable home is based on Moore's memories of his own family's house in Clifton Street.

Judith Hearne is a victim of forces beyond her control, and her self-delusion and snobbery are all that keep her afloat. She worships the bullying parish priest Father Quigley while looking down on the professor's kindly wife Moira. Her busybody landlady Mrs Rice and pampered son Bernard are unpleasant characters, as are her fellow lodgers, but one seems different. James Patrick Madden is uneducated and loudly dressed, but unlike every other man, he does not reject Judith at first glance. He is a recently returned emigrant, having spent most of his working life in New York, 'in the hotel business right on Times Square', as he puts it. With his brash manners Madden is out of place in Belfast, but Miss Hearne recognizes that underneath his bluster he is as lonely as she is. She begins to dream of marrying him and finding the security and happiness she craves, until the illusions that have sustained her are punctured one by one.

The sense of desperation in *The Lonely Passion of Judith Hearne* is set alongside nuanced observations and moments of pure social comedy. The landlady's morning hair, 'sticking out from her head like a forkful of wet hay', a dejected greyhound 'moving his tiny padded feet in discomfort at the cold' and the damp misery of Belfast are conveyed brilliantly, and we feel the texture of a life lived out in this unfriendly environment. The almost invisible Miss Hearne becomes a woman who refuses to be ignored, with a voice that becomes more honest and braver, never more so than when she has nothing left to lose. As Diana Athill says, Moore's view of life in this novel is tragic, 'but one that does not make a fuss about tragedy, accepting it as part of the fabric with which we all have to make do'. Judith Hearne has something in common with that other flawed literary heroine, Emma Bovary. We sympathize with her, not for her likeability, but because of the way that Moore captures her inner life.

Graham Greene called Brian Moore his favourite living novelist, and it's easy to see why: Moore's nineteen novels range from political parables to metaphysical thrillers and historical fiction. His best novels, for me, are the ones that centre on a woman's consciousness, including *I Am Mary Dunne* (1968), *The Doctor's Wife* (1976) and his last published novel, *The Magician's Wife* (1997).

Apart from occasional visits, Moore never went back to Belfast, and he spent most of his later life writing in relative seclusion in California with his second wife Jean. Even though he became internationally famous, and won many literary honours, he was not always recognized in his native Ireland. He told the story of how, in the 1990s, he went into a bookshop in Dublin and asked if they had anything 'by the Irish writer, Brian Moore'. No, the assistant said, after checking the computer, but they did have several novels by a Canadian writer of that name.

Moore might feel differently about the welcoming, cosmopolitan city that is Belfast today. Go and see it for yourself if you can: the Lough and surrounding hills look beautiful in the sunshine after the rainclouds have passed. Moore wrote his essay 'Going Home' after visiting the grave of a long-dead family friend in Connemara. There, looking out to sea, it struck him that, after a lifetime of travelling, he had made his peace with Ireland. 'And in that moment I know that when I die, I would like to come home at last to be buried here in this quiet place among the grazing cows.' It was the last essay he wrote, published posthumously in February 1999.

ANN KENNEDY SMITH is a writer and biographer. She moved to England at the age of 23 but goes back to Northern Ireland as often as she can.

Fabulous Beasts

ALAN BRADLEY

It is a commonplace of detection that the best place to hide something is in plain view. When it comes to books, this means reading the parts we normally skip. In my 1794 edition of Fanny Burney's novel *Camilla* there is a list, as was the custom at the time, of those who subscribed to the cost of the initial printing. Among all the now forgotten His and Her Graces, the Gentlemen and Ladies, are listed Warren Hastings, the Rt. Hon. Edmund Burke ('5 copies'), and one J. Austen, Steventon. You have only to pause for a moment over those names and you have opened the door to an adventure in detection.

Detection also involves imagination. I remember coming across a paperback poetry collection in an Oxfam shop which was inscribed with undying love for the recipient on her birthday. Yet there it was, only two or three years later, banished to a charity-shop shelf. What went wrong? Was it a comedy or a tragedy?

My most spine-tingling find, however, was a copy of Sir John Harington's translation of Ariosto's *Orlando Furioso*. It was published in 1591 and reprinted in 1607. The story goes that, as well as inventing the water closet, Sir John translated the raciest section of the epic poem to titillate the ladies at Court. On discovering this, Elizabeth I commanded him as punishment to translate all 46 cantos. The title page of my copy is missing and the corners of some other pages have been rubbed away by earlier hands, but inscribed inside the cover are the words: 'This book was bought at the sale of the effects of Lady

Christopher de Hamel, *Meetings with Remarkable Manuscripts* (2016)
Allen Lane · Hb · 640pp · £30 · ISBN 9780241003046

Eleanor Butler and Miss Ponsonby at Plasanwyd [*sic*] Llangollen and valued as the second edition by the Ladies (July 1832).'

Lady Eleanor was the lifelong companion of Sarah Ponsonby, and their elopement and subsequent lives are described in Elizabeth Mavor's bestselling *The Ladies of Llangollen* (1971) where I also found their portraits. That in itself is fascinating enough, but, when I pick it up, my imagination doesn't stop with the Ladies but flies back to the sixteenth century, when it was first on a bookseller's table in Elizabethan London. Perhaps Ben Jonson picked up this very copy and leafed through it, maybe even Shakespeare himself turned over a few pages. After all, part of the plot of *Much Ado about Nothing* is pinched from *Orlando Furioso* . . .

Printed books are within reach of us all, but go back a couple more centuries to a time before the invention of printing, and the best most of us can hope for is to see a single manuscript page displayed in a locked glass cabinet in a library or a museum. There may be an exquisite illustration of an imaginary beast peering out at us from behind a letter, and we long to touch it and turn the page. Recently the British Library and the French Bibliothèque Nationale have copied and put their manuscript treasures on line, so it's possible to browse page by page. But there can be nothing like the experience of touching the parchment itself.

There are a few scholars who are fortunate enough to be able to do so, to feel the texture of the page, to hold a magnifying glass over the brilliant illuminations by the mostly unknown monks who created them. But these experts are on the whole a reclusive lot, their studies appearing in learned journals which most of us never see. So it is a huge pleasure to discover that one of them has written a book for the common reader, profusely illustrated in vibrant colour, albeit not of facsimile quality (and just as important, not at a facsimile price).

Christopher de Hamel's *Meetings with Remarkable Manuscripts* (2016) is a joy. The binding, the layout and the lavish illustration make it a pleasure to handle before you even turn to the content, which perfectly fulfils its promise. De Hamel's writing is not academic but vivid and entertaining, while the coloured reproductions are almost as dazzling as the fabulous beasts which so often clamber around their margins. As he says in his introduction, 'the chapters are not unlike a series of celebrity interviews'.

Nor do you simply meet these extraordinary manuscripts: you walk with him into the libraries where they dwell. Some libraries are remarkably helpful and easily accessible, leaving him for hours alone with the text, his pen and his notebook. Others are more like high-security prisons where, having been admitted through a series of locked doors and escorted down long corridors, he finally reaches the cell in which the precious text has been placed ready on a table, and the interview takes place under the hawk-like gaze of a guard.

The Hunterian Psalter, Glasgow

Each encounter becomes a detective story as he examines the way in which the book was put together and tries to uncover as much information as possible about the scribes who wrote and illustrated it. This painstaking process reveals that 'the manuscript has a persona, an identity and very often a name which subsequently stays with it forever. It is curious how assigning names to particular manuscripts gives them a character as with domestic animals.' *The Book of Kells* was so named in 1620 and it has been called that ever since.

The less memorably named *Codex Amiatinus* is one of the dozen remarkable creatures de Hamel encounters. This is the oldest surviving text of the Vulgate (St Jerome's Latin translation of the Bible), and since the end of the eighteenth century it has lived in the Biblioteca Laurenziana in Florence. Yet it was created in England, copied from a text lent to the monasteries of Jarrow and Wearmouth by Rome sometime around AD 700. The monks made three copies:

one for each monastery and one to go back to Rome. This was often the way in which the loan of a text was repaid: by providing a copy.

This one in Florence is the only survivor. It contains the oldest English painting to which any absolute date can be assigned (that is, not later than AD 716). Bede knew of the book and wrote about it. The monk Ceolfrith was given the task of escorting this copy back to Rome. However, he died on the way and the book was stranded for a while in France. In 1036 it is recorded as being in the San Salvatore Monastery in Italy and as being 'written in the hand of the blessed Pope Gregory'. (Apparently it was quite common to ascribe the writing of texts to Pope Gregory.) De Hamel unravels its wandering journey from Jarrow to Florence and along the way uncovers much about the times it lived through and the people it met.

It is still bound in one volume (as Bede recorded back in England in the eighth century) which is 11 1/2 inches thick and about 20 inches tall. Before opening it de Hamel has to ask for other books to rest it on to avoid straining the spine. This being one of the friendlier libraries where he is left alone with the volume (apart from the occasional person popping in to use the photocopier), he is able to try picking it up and discovers that, using both arms, he can just lift it. From a previous interviewer, who took some scales to meet the *Codex* fifty years before this visit, he has already learned that it weighs around 90lb – 'about the weight of a fully grown female adult Great Dane'.

By the end of his adventures with the twelve manuscripts he describes one's spirit is aflame and it's not hard to imagine taking seriously his exhortations to go further. 'There are good careers in manuscript studies in rare book libraries, universities and the antiquarian book trade, but there are opportunities too for perceptive enthusiasts, textual editors, private collectors, scribes, artists and readers, exactly as there have been for a thousand years.'

For a professional's view you can read C. J. Wright's 'Confessions of a Manuscripts' Curator' in *SF* no. 23. But you can also take up Christopher de Hamel's challenge to seek out treasures for yourself.

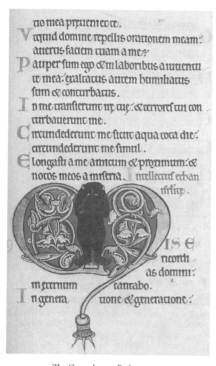

The Copenhagen Psalter

He estimates that there are probably upwards of a million medieval manuscripts waiting to be discovered in libraries, local museums and country houses. Most of them won't have glorious imaginary beasts painted in their margins, but they are themselves wonderful beasts and not imaginary at all, just hiding in plain view waiting to reveal their secrets. And according to de Hamel, you may even be able to buy a page of a thirteenth-century Bible for less than the price of a good theatre ticket.

Finally, a word of warning. If you decide to buy this wonderful book, do make sure to buy the hardback version. The Penguin paperback may be cheaper, but it has been reduced in size, and though the cover is in colour, all the illustrations inside are in black-and-white, which largely takes away its point.

ALAN BRADLEY takes great delight in a local book auction where, even if he can't afford to buy, he can pat and greet some remarkable beasts on their way to new homes.

Portrait of the Artist in Middle Age

WILLIAM PALMER

Like many men now in their seventies, I have suffered from Sudden Accidental Reflection Syndrome. It can be upsetting. Most men have, until their first exposure to it, lived with the easy and comforting assumption that inwardly they remain about thirty-five, even if they are twice that age. They keep reasonably fit, they don't smoke or drink too much, or dress their age; all the things their fathers did before them. Day by day they discount the erosions of age hinted at in their shaving mirrors: those, that is, who have not adopted the comforting hedge of a beard. But one fateful day as they advance confidently along the pavement and wait for a lull in the traffic, there comes an awful collision, not physical, but none the less shattering: they cross the road and see advancing towards them an irritatingly undodgeable old fool, and realize this man is their unsuspected, horribly real self reflected in the plate-glass window of a shopfront.

To the novelist Evelyn Waugh, such a moment helped to precipitate a mental breakdown and to inspire his autobiographical novel *The Ordeal of Gilbert Pinfold*. It came very early: he was only 50 in 1953, and at the height of his fame as a bestselling and critically acclaimed novelist, but he was also a man who preferred to live in almost Victorian seclusion in his country house with his family.

In that year he celebrated – if that's the word – Christmas at home. He had been unwell and depressed for some time. Chronic insomnia was only partially alleviated by drugs and alcohol. The tax man and

Evelyn Waugh, *The Ordeal of Gilbert Pinfold* (1957)
Penguin · Pb · 208pp · £9.99 · ISBN 9780141184500

rheumatism plagued him. His memory had begun to play alarming, vividly detailed tricks. But let Waugh's account, only lightly fictionalized from his own life, take up the story:

> The children's holidays were a time when Mr Pinfold felt a special need for unconsciousness at night and for stimulated geniality by day. Christmas was always the worst season. During that dread week he made copious use of wine and narcotics and his inflamed face shone like the florid squireens depicted in the cards that littered the house. Once catching sight of himself in the looking-glass, thus empurpled and wearing a paper crown, he took fright at what he saw.
> 'I must get away,' said Mr Pinfold later to his wife.

To judge by Waugh's letters and journals and the accounts of his friends, this was a pretty accurate description of Waugh's own state. To try to recover his health, he booked a passage on a cruise ship, the *Staffordshire*, that was to sail through the Mediterranean and the Suez Canal and across the Indian Ocean to what was then Ceylon.

There is no direct contemporaneous record of what happened to Waugh while he was travelling, except for a few cables and letters he sent to his wife Laura. These were alarming enough, complaining of a devilish conspiracy against him involving the use of radio waves and telepathy. When he came home he was profoundly shaken and he did not begin the novel until 1956.

As *The Ordeal* opens, Gilbert Pinfold is a successful novelist in his late forties, but looking and feeling much older. He lives comfortably in the country with his wife and children. He does not consider himself rich but he can afford servants and good wine. Even so things are not going well. 'He had become lazy . . . he spent most of the day in an armchair. He ate less, drank more and grew corpulent . . .' Not surprisingly, indolence and indulgence mean that his health is not good and the lack of daily activity causes him to suffer from chronic insomnia.

Creative work uses only a small part of the day and for the rest he is 'merely bored'. His trips to the outside world are mostly confined to London, where he gets drunk in visits to his clubs and to old friends and is uncomfortably conscious that he has developed an unpleasant persona somewhere between 'eccentric don and testy colonel'.

After the Christmas fright, he is relieved to join his cruise. His ship, ominously, is called the *Caliban*. Pinfold feels a little better as he settles into his cabin. He is a good sailor and even when the steward who brings his tea tells him that many of his fellow passengers are seasick, Pinfold goes out to take the air.

The main deck, when he reached it, was almost deserted. Two wind-blown girls in thick sweaters were tacking along arm-in-arm past the piles of folded chairs. Mr Pinfold hobbled to the after smoking-room bar. Four or five men sat together in one corner. He nodded to them, found a chair on the further side and ordered brandy and ginger-ale . . . After a time two cheer-ful women entered. The men greeted them . . . Mr Pinfold studied this group with benevolence.

Little does poor Mr Pinfold realize that he is shortly to be plunged into hell. When he returns to his cabin after lunch he is dismayed by the very loud playing of a jazz band in the next-door cabin. When that ceases he hears what he identifies as a dog pattering about in the corridor. The young man in the next cabin denies possessing either a gramophone or a dog. When Pinfold wakes during the night a religious service is taking place below his cabin. These sounds, he becomes convinced, must be the result of some sort of faulty public-address system. Perhaps the vessel had been a troopship and still has remnants of the intercom installed to make announcements to crew and passengers. But then the voices start . . .

Two elderly generals discuss Pinfold's drunkenness; two young men accuse him of being an impostor, a homosexual, a hypocrite in his religion, a coward in his war service, impotent, a cheat and thief, and they threaten to give him a good thrashing. One thing Pinfold certainly is not is a coward. When the young men challenge him through the lamp on his table at dinner, Pinfold barks back at the lamp, challenging them to meet him and have it out like men . . . No one appears at the rendezvous Pinfold has chosen for a showdown. When he is attempting to sleep the voices wake him. When he is up and about they follow him, and when they are absent he imagines that the ordinary (visible) passengers are audibly whispering about him. Even when the ship docks, voices follow him on to land. The persecution is incessant, though Pinfold does fight back by finding the most boring book he can in the ship's library, Charles Kingsley's *Westward Ho!*, and reading it aloud to them until they ask for mercy.

It wouldn't be fair to the prospective reader to give away the twists and turns of Pinfold's often blackly comic fight against his pursuing demons. But the end is a happy and surprisingly tender one.

Waugh was not generally a man to put himself into his own fiction and *The Ordeal* came as a surprise when it was published in 1957, as it was quite obviously an unsparing self-portrait. (The short, tubby, formally dressed figure shown on the dust jacket as unsteadily emerging on two sticks from the flames of hell should have killed any further doubt.) All autobiographical fiction is more or less than the truth, but the tale of Pinfold does appear very close to the one Waugh told to his friends. Frances Donaldson, in her book *Evelyn Waugh: Portrait of a Country Neighbour*, recounts how after his return and recovery, Waugh related his hallucinations with detachment and much self-mockery: 'all the actual happenings and incidents he described in detail are in the book as close to reality as suits the convention of a novel'. Indeed, Waugh acknowledged in a famous television interview with John Freeman that what happens to Gilbert Pinfold in the novel had been suffered by himself at far greater length and severity, but that it would have been both boring and inartistic to include every detail.

The sufferings of Mr Pinfold do not invite our pity. Waugh was not a man who usually sought or inspired thoughts of pity or emotional empathy but what strikes one in reading the novel, and Waugh's journals, is his utter honesty about himself. Despite the carapace he developed and the off-putting coldness shown to anyone he considered his social or intellectual inferior, he appears as a man morbidly unsure of himself, beset by suspicion of antagonistic conspiracies and a real fear of madness.

For a writer who guarded his private life and cultivated a sometimes deliberately offensive public figure it was an extraordinary book to produce. But writers, who are often accused of using or misusing their families and friends in their work, are only truly honest if they can sacrifice themselves to their art. Novelists with an abiding interest in themselves as their subject matter are usually second-rate. Waugh was never that. He knew a good story when he saw one, even if he was the butt of it.

The Ordeal of Gilbert Pinfold is a very dark comedy, but there is a touching nobility in its hero striding out at night to confront the host of enemies awaiting him on deck:

> the ship came to life with a multitude of voices. This, Mr Pinfold decided, was his moment to act . . . Gripping his blackthorn he left the cabin.
>
> Immediately his communications were cut. The lighted corridor was empty and completely silent. He strode down it to the stairway, mounted to the main deck. No one was about . . . not a light anywhere on the dark horizon; not a sound from the bridge; only the rush and slap of the waves along the ship's side, and the keen sea wind. Mr Pinfold stood confounded, the only troubled thing in a world at peace.

WILLIAM PALMER is currently finishing a study of twentieth-century alcoholic writers entitled *In Love with Hell*. He is as paranoiac as the next writer, but not yet to a Pinfoldian extent.

Gone Fishing

MARY HELEN SPOONER

My father departed this world via Lake Michigan, during a salmon fishing jamboree sponsored by his camping club. He and my mother had pulled an Airstream travel trailer from their home in St Louis, and shortly after arrival met a man carrying an impressive catch. The fellow camper pointed out the pier where he had been fishing, and my father immediately grabbed his gear and headed to the site.

Witnesses said he either slipped or was knocked into the water by a wave. But there was no sign of him for a full week, and during this period my sisters and I imagined our father, who always carried a pocket knife, drifting to another shore, disoriented and perhaps living in the woods as a bearded wild man. Or floating out of Lake Michigan through the canals and other Great Lakes to the St Lawrence Seaway and the Atlantic, which seemed a fitting end for a man afflicted with a bad case of wanderlust. His body was eventually discovered on the lake shore some distance from the campsite, blessed by a priest, cremated and his ashes sent back to St Louis.

A few months before his death I gave my father a copy of the *Collected Poems of Robert Service*, a British-Canadian poet whose long ballads he had discovered in his younger, single days while working on building sites in Alaska and Canada. He spoke often of his favourite, 'The Cremation of Sam McGee', about a gold miner in the Yukon who honours his dying fellow prospector's request for cremation rather than interment in a frozen grave. Hauling Sam McGee's

---

Collected Poems of Robert Service (1993) is out of print but we can try to obtain second-hand copies.

44

body for days on a dog sled, the narrator eventually finds a wrecked boat along a lake shore and uses it as a makeshift crematorium.

My father had never owned a copy of the book but remembered the story and could recall lines from the poem, recited to him by other construction workers he met in those northern territories. The narrator opens the cabin of the boat to check on the cremation's progress, only to discover Sam basking in the heat, 'and he wore a smile you could see a mile and he said, please shut that door'.

Robert Service was born in Preston, Lancashire, on 16 January 1874, one of ten children of a Scottish postal worker and his wife. He was educated in Glasgow, then worked as a bank clerk and managed to complete one term at the University of Glasgow. He found publishers for his early verses in the *Glasgow Herald* and local magazines. But he longed for adventure and began saving as much as he could for a passage to western Canada, where he planned to become a cowboy. He travelled by ship to Montreal and by train to British Columbia, where he spent over a year working on farms and ranches. Still restless, he caught a boat from Vancouver Island to Seattle, then wandered down to California and Mexico and spent two more years working at a series of odd jobs and exploring the western United States. He would later recall a youthful ambition to be an American hobo, but he only indulged in spells of vagrancy, and even in his leanest moments he kept 'ten cents between myself and the wolf'.

Service returned to Victoria and found work at the Canadian Bank of Commerce, which later transferred him to the town of Whitehorse, in Yukon territory. The local minister was famous for having cooked and eaten his sealskin boots to avoid starvation when lost on a trail to Fort McPherson, and he hosted Saturday night gatherings in the church hall, where guests were invited to make their own entertainment. Service would recite Rudyard Kipling's 'Gunga Din' and other works of narrative verse, and he had some of his own published in the local newspaper, the *White Horse Star*. He had been trying to compose something with a local theme, then, during an evening walk, he heard raucous sounds coming from the local bars. Service, who rarely drank alcohol, said that the opening line of one of his best-known poems, 'The Shooting of Dan McGrew', immediately popped into his mind: 'A bunch of the boys were whooping it up in the Malamute saloon'.

He did not go home that night but went to his desk at the bank and wrote out his first long ballad, about a mysterious stranger and a local card player who kill each other over a woman. It was deemed inappropriate for a church social entertainment, but nearly a century later 'The Shooting of Dan McGrew' would be recited at Buckingham Palace by Ronald Reagan and the Canadian Prime Minister Brian Mulroney at a post-summit dinner, when they learned that the Queen and the Queen Mother were also Robert Service fans.

'The Cremation of Sam McGee' soon followed, when a prospector told him an improbable tale of a miner who had cremated his friend in the wild. Service was enthralled by the story, and later said he composed the poem in his mind while walking local trails in the moonlight. The creative floodgates had opened, and when he felt he had enough verses for a book he sent them to his father (who had also emigrated) in Toronto, along with a cheque, and asked him to have them printed. He imagined that *Songs of a Sourdough* would be a kind of vanity undertaking, and that the printed copies would make Christmas gifts for his friends.

Service's father took the poems to the Methodist Book and Publishing House, where they were a big hit with the staff. Word of mouth generated 1,700 pre-orders, and the publisher posted Service's cheque back to him, along with a royalty contract for the book. Any misgivings the Methodist publisher may have had over Service's earthy ballads were overridden by the fact that *Songs of a Sourdough* (1907) had already become a bestseller. Within the year there were editions printed in New York and London, and the book was subsequently reprinted many times.

In 1908 the bank transferred Service to Dawson City, a Yukon town that had been the centre of the Klondike Gold Rush. By then he had become a Yukon celebrity, but according to one biographer, 'he slid into town one day without any great fanfare, and was soon to be seen weighing out gold dust in the tellers' cage of the Canadian Bank of Commerce on Front Street'. Visitors wanting to catch a glimpse of him were surprised to see 'a shy and nondescript man in his mid-thirties, with a fresh complexion, clear blue eyes and a boyish figure that made him look younger'. His speech was described as having 'an English inflection, and an American drawl and Scottish overtones'.

The gold boom had ended a decade earlier, but there were plenty of miners still in the area with tales to tell, and Service quickly produced another collection of verses, *Ballads of a Cheechako* (1909), which included works with such titles as 'The Ballad of Blasphemous Bill' and 'Claw-fingered Kitty'. 'Cheechako' was the local term for a newcomer to Alaska or the Yukon territory.

Service then resigned from his bank job, moved to a rustic cabin on a hill and devoted himself to writing novels. In 1912 he accepted a job with the *Toronto*

Service served as a Red Cross ambulance driver in France during the First World War. Reproduced by courtesy of Anne Longepe, Robert W. Service Estate

Star as a correspondent in Europe, later basing himself in Paris and then in Brittany. He spent part of the Second World War in Hollywood, where he was given a one-line part in a film with John Wayne and Marlene Dietrich and where his first novel, *The Trail of Ninety-Eight* (1909), was made into a film. After the war he returned to France, where he continued to write until his death in 1958.

Service's verse is often dismissed as doggerel, and derivative of some of Kipling's works, but his popularity endures. The late US Senator John McCain spoke of learning 'The Cremation of Sam

McGee' from a fellow captive when he was a prisoner-of-war in Vietnam. And a recording Johnny Cash made of the poem was discovered in a cache of unreleased tapes shortly after his death, which were then compiled into a two-disc set, *Personal File*. A reviewer for US National Public Radio described Cash's interpretation of the poem as the 'standout moment' in the collection, with the country singer lending the work the gravitas it needed.

When I gave my father Service's *Collected Poems*, he immediately began memorizing 'The Cremation of Sam McGee', hoping to recite it at parties. He would bring the book out after a meal, a family friend later told me, and say, 'Let's have a poem!' I badly wanted to read it at his funeral, but my mother would not hear of it, sending me and another sister to confer with her priest about suitable biblical quotations. But I put *Collected Poems of Robert Service* into my shoulder bag and at the reception after mass I spoke to the funeral director. He thought it a wonderful idea and announced to the guests that I had something to share.

'I am going to read you something my father was learning,' I told them, 'something you likely would have heard had he been with us here.' I began reading, and my 7-year-old nephew ran over to me, exclaiming that he remembered the poem. I put my arm round his shoulders, and we read it aloud together:

> There are strange things done in the midnight sun
> By the men who moil for gold;
> The Arctic trails have their secret tales
> That would make your blood run cold;
> The Northern Lights have seen queer sights,
> But the queerest they ever did see
> Was that night on the marge of Lake Lebarge
> I cremated Sam McGee.

MARY HELEN SPOONER, who has inherited her father's wanderlust, worked as a journalist in Latin America for many years.

Betrayals

CHRISTOPHER RUSH

I have a Russian wife. We work together – articles, talks, translations, books, to keep the wolf from the door. Sometimes, when a bigger than usual energy bill slides through the letterbox, or the car breaks down or the tax-man cometh, one of us will look at the other with a rueful grin and say: 'The solution as I see it, Comrade, is to work harder.'

It's a direct quotation from *Animal Farm* (1945) and the character we are quoting is the big carthorse Boxer, eighteen hands high, and the stalwart representative of the proletariat in George Orwell's book. The quip consists in the fact that merely to work harder is not the solution. Nor was it the answer to the problems faced by the Russian people in the wake of the 1917 Revolution and the era of Lenin and Stalin. But Boxer's faith in hard work is as admirable as his fate is shocking, and for all the story's humour, it is Boxer who gives it its tragic centre and its emotional power.

Most of us have read *Animal Farm*. We all know pretty well what it is: a satirical allegory in the form of a fable, and a parable on the history of Communist Russia from the 1917 Revolution to the end of 1943. That would be my literary definition, to which I would add that the book also has a wider symbolic purpose. In other words it's about the Revolution but that's not all it's about. And while we know what the book's about, what should be better known is how difficult it was for Orwell to get it published. One American publisher rejected it

George Orwell, *Animal Farm: A Fairy Story* (1945)
Penguin · Pb · 144pp · £8.99 · ISBN 9780141182704

because he said there was no real market for animal stories. And even after it was published some bookshops placed it in the children's section.

You could of course argue that Orwell had nobody but himself to blame, because he called it *Animal Farm: A Fairy Story*, an ironic subtitle to say the least. But any bookseller with a grain of sense should have recognized at once that the 'fairy story' possessed a meaning far beyond talking animals and fantastic situations. In the Grey Rabbit stories the weasel and the fox are simply villains and Hare is simply selfish and self-important; the cooking-pot and the red-hot oven are terrifying enough but they are what they are and no more; and when the owl bites off Grey Rabbit's tail and bandages the bleeding stump with a cobweb there is nothing behind it but some nostalgic rustic lore, beloved of Alison Uttley. With Orwell it's something else again.

Most publishers naturally saw all too well that the clarity of the writing and the simplicity of the storyline, the characters and situations, circumstances and events were exact allegorical equivalents of the Russian Revolution and its betrayal by Stalin and his henchmen for their own selfish ends. To anyone who possessed the faintest knowledge of Russian and European history from 1917 to 1943, the book unrolled like a chart of correspondences, crystal clear. As follows:

Manor Farm is Tsarist Russia, Animal Farm is Russia after the Revolution, later recognized as the Soviet Union; Mr Jones is the Tsar, Nicholas II; the humans are the capitalist ruling class; the animals are the working classes in general, and the pigs the post-Revolution totalitarian rulers. Specifically Old Major is a combination of Marx and Lenin. Snowball is Trotsky, expelled and assassinated, with Napoleon as Stalin, Squealer his spin doctor, the dogs his secret police, the pigeons his spies, and the bleating sheep the mindless mob. Jones's expulsion is the Bolshevik Revolution; his return the Counter-Revolution; the Battle of the Cowshed its defeat, with the Battle of the Windmill being the German invasion of Russia in 1941, and Stalingrad. There is Moses the raven, who represents the Church; Boxer and Clover the proletariat in particular; the principles of Animalism are those of Marxism/Communism; the Windmill Plan is the inauguration of the five-year plans; the hens are the kulaks, and their refusal to hand over their eggs the real kulaks' destruction of their own farms to avoid the state getting its hands on them.

Orwell did not stop there. The animal slaughters are the fake trials and forced confessions and bloody purges ordered by Stalin in the 1920s and 1930s. Neighbouring farms and their owners are easily identifiable. Pilkington is Churchill, his Foxwood farm, Britain; Frederick is Hitler and his Pinchfield Germany. Even the non-aggression pact is there, and the breaking of it by Hitler. Finally Napoleon's party, where pigs and men meet and cheat, represents the meeting between Stalin, Churchill and Roosevelt at the Tehran Conference of 1943. When at the end Squealer is seen walking on his two hind legs and Napoleon carries a whip in his trotter, the story of equivalences is all but complete. One set of masters has been replaced by another, and the central principle has been hideously corrupted and perverted; all animals are equal but some animals are more equal than others. The oppressed animals, terrorized by their own kind, look from pig to man and man to pig, and from pig to man again, and can no longer tell the difference. 'It was impossible to say which was which.' Stalin and Stalinism had triumphed and an entire nation had been betrayed.

The artistic ease and sheer simplicity with which Orwell arranges it all, with a farm as his setting, ought to have astonished publishers into acceptance. In fact Gollancz sent it back stating that it was impossible for him to publish such a book: Stalin after all was an ally. He wasn't the only one unwilling to risk offending Uncle Joe, of whom Churchill himself had said that it was better to have him on the inside pissing out than on the outside pissing in. Jonathan Cape turned it down next, and so did T. S. Eliot at Faber, who had already rejected *Down and Out in Paris and London* a dozen years previously.

As for *Animal Farm* he thought that it was the wrong time, the wrong point of view, that it was simply too negative. And so on. Sadly, Eliot wrote Orwell a chilly rejection which said that as the pigs were obviously far more intelligent than any of the other animals, clearly they were best qualified to manage the farm.

So far as Orwell was concerned these attitudes were anti-libertarian because, as he had written in his proposed but omitted preface, 'Many of our intellectuals have accepted the principle that a book should be published or suppressed, praised or damned, not on its merits but according to political expediency' – an outright denial of Voltaire's famous principle: 'I detest what you say but I will defend to the death your right to say it.' And Orwell went on to say with blunt clarity: 'If liberty means anything at all, it means the right to tell people what they do not want to hear.' Eventually Frederic Warburg accepted it and it went on to sell at ten times the rate Orwell was used to. It appeared in the USA a year later, and by the end of the decade well over half a million copies had been sold. Truth had triumphed, and so had the book.

The book itself, though anti-Stalinist, is not narrowly anti-Soviet, though that is its primary intention, but is a comment on all revolutions which bring to power power-hungry people who eventually pervert the ideals with which a revolution starts out and become the new masters, like Napoleon, with whips in their trotters. What is it that goes wrong? Human nature – it simply gets in the way of revolutionary ideals. The masses aren't alert enough to know or to say when enough is enough. And the power-seekers are all too ready to take advantage of this, and to take control.

Some critics think the comic sense is so great in this book – no apparent Orwellian bitterness or despair – that it almost lulls you into non-awareness of its political message. And certainly there are some things in it that encourage us to enjoy the book purely for the skill and charm and fun of it: the various animal committees – the Clean Tails League for Cows, for example – and scenes such as the cat sitting up on the roof of the barn and graciously inviting any sparrow who chooses to come and perch on her paw because all animals are now comrades (the sparrows keep their distance!). But for my money it's not the smiling book some say it is. The rage may be muted beneath the laughter, but it is there. And in no part of the book more so than in the story of what happened to Boxer, the loyal worker sold to the knacker and slaughtered in his yard when no more work can be got out of his battered old carcass. As Malcom Bradbury commented, tanks may crush people and ayatollahs and imams and state leaders offer bribes of half a bushel of apples to sell out the Boxers of this world. But Boxer will not be airbrushed from history. Orwell has seen to that.

Boxer's death is in fact the emotional climax of the book. He is the salt-of-the-earth – good, honest, hard-working, selfless and decent. He gives his all – and all for others, for the cause. Hence the terrible circumstances of his betrayal. It could have been avoided, had the animals stood their ground at the start and prevented the pigs from taking over. The story is about the awful consequences of passivity and blind faith. The cynical and ruthless slaughter of the good but gullible workhorse in the knacker's yard is the most powerful and shocking moment of the narrative. But this is what people do to people; this, more specifically, is what dictators do to their own people. They betray them. *Animal Farm* is ultimately about this betrayal, about the betrayal of individuals and ideals, and of entire nations. If satire is the exposure of the frailty of human institutions through laughter, indignation or contempt, there is no truer or greater satire than *Animal Farm*.

CHRISTOPHER RUSH has been writing for thirty-five years. His books include the memoirs *To Travel Hopefully* and *Hellfire and Herring*, and *Will*, a novel about Shakespeare. His latest novel, *Penelope's Web*, was published in 2015.

A Hardy Perennial

ISABEL LLOYD

The summer of 2018 was a glory – as long as you weren't a gardener. For those of us who fret about plants, it was a season as much to be endured as enjoyed. After a cold, late spring, the weather had pulled a U-turn, swerving into an intense dry heat that lasted from June to the end of August. With 7 per cent less rain than even the summer of '76 – still, after a whole series of climatic upheavals, the touchstone for freak British weather – it wasn't so surprising that anything newly planted shrivelled in the furnace. More shocking was the number of weighty, established plants that turned their faces to the wall. In my garden in Sussex we lost shrubs and trees that had been happy and healthy for twenty years: Korean lilac, a beautiful *Exochorda x macrantha* 'The Bride', pompom willows, a huge evergreen elaeagnus. Clumps of tickweed flopped; what should have been giant angelica, sown in hope a year before, couldn't drag itself higher than a few inches off the ground.

Sadly, the Englishwoman best placed to cope with and comment on conditions like these wasn't around to see them. Beth Chatto, gardener, writer and popularizer of the motto 'the right plant in the right place', had died that May, at the excellent age of 94. Regardless of both the weather and Chatto's departure, her famous garden and its associated nursery bloomed on. As you would expect: its creator

---

Beth Chatto, *The Dry Garden* (1978, rev. ed. 2018)
Weidenfeld & Nicolson · Pb · 288pp · £9.99 · ISBN 9781474610964
The Beth Chatto Gardens and Nursery are open to visitors; for more details see www.bethchatto.co.uk.

wrote what has been for four decades the go-to text for anyone who knows what it is to look at the sky and pray for a drop of rain.

The Dry Garden, Chatto's first book, was published in 1978, two years after that earlier record-breaking summer. It offered gardeners who'd come to hate the sight of a hose 180-odd pages of drought-beating design, planting and maintenance advice. Crucially, this was based on experience hard-won after what was then already nearly forty years of nurturing plants in East Anglia, England's driest corner. Within two years the book had been reprinted, and it went on appearing in regular reissues and revisions until the late 1990s, when other, showier garden writers moved centre-stage. Then in 2018 Weidenfeld & Nicolson published the first new edition in twenty years – just as the weather, finally, broke. A case, you might say, of the right book at the right time.

It was as much fashion as timeliness that made *The Dry Garden* a success. Chatto had spent the 1950s teaching flower-arranging, was close friends with a local grandee artist and plantsman, Sir Cedric Morris, and was married to an amateur but passionate botanist. All of which had helped form her particular gardening style. She laid out beds with an aristocratically generous sense of space; planted them with a florist's knack for first setting up a geometry, then breaking it (she was particularly fond of arranging plants in three-dimensional, interlocking triangles); and used an enormous range of what were then often unfamiliar shrubs and perennials. The results were flowing, rhythmical and always at home in their space: a good fit for the new wave of naturalistic gardening that was sluicing away the prim rockeries and garish bedding of the 1960s.

Chatto's insistence on matching plants to the conditions that best suited them also chimed with more nature-friendly times: the Soil Association, the charity devoted to promoting organic farming and gardening, had been launched just five years previously. Meanwhile her European travels with that botanizing husband, observing plants in unforgiving habitats like the sunbaked, stony hillsides of southern

France, meant she properly understood what they needed to thrive. As a nurserywoman she was always assiduous in searching out, growing and recommending new plants that would cope with, even revel in, the most difficult of conditions.

Gardeners came to love and rely on her because what she said worked, and her 'right plant for the right place' mantra became so widely adopted it's now a cliché. Like all commonplaces, it's a pearl of wisdom laid around a central grit of truth. One of the first but sometimes hardest lessons for beginner gardeners is that fighting Nature is a losing game: trying to keep a moisture-loving plant alive in arid soils is both back- and heart-breaking. Chatto's lifelong focus on the botany of the plants she grew meant she could avoid this kind of unnecessary pain and teach her readers how to avoid it too.

Even in the slow-moving world of horticulture, forty years is a long time: our tastes in gardens, and in books, have moved on. Contemporary gardening titles tend to be big on visuals, light on actual advice. That is not the Chatto way. *The Dry Garden* is a plain child. Illustrations are confined to hand-drawn ground plans, a few marginally more elegant black-and-white line drawings, and a handful of unenlightening monochrome photos, mostly close-ups of plants Chatto particularly valued. In his introduction to the new edition of *The Dry Garden*, the writer and broadcaster Monty Don says: 'at a time when gardening could sometimes seem to be a cross between an exercise in good taste and Latin O level, Beth made it a creative adventure'. True. But if you want to join her on that journey, you'll have to take your own pictures.

As for Latin, like all good horticulturalists – who value precision – Chatto insisted on using the full, Latin botanical names for all the plants she wrote about. But she does seem less concerned about taste, at least not the kind that is an exercise in fitting a template – she says she groups plants in beds according to their shape and character, leaving their flower colour to an atypically jokey aside: 'Colour schemes often seem to make themselves!' That thrumming noise you can hear is Vita Sackville-West, creator of Sissinghurst and colour-scheme obsessive-in-chief, gyrating in her grave.

When it comes to what the book has to teach, there's still an abundance to enjoy. It begins with general but still useful advice about judging soil and climate. This quickly sidesteps into considerations about the challenges of Chatto's own site – in 1958, an unpromising stretch of uncultivated sand, gravel, silty mud and bracken. Gardeners are nosy creatures, so this and all her other dips into the personal are gratifying. Then we get into moisture conservation ('I really don't hold with watering'), planting, fertilizing ('we turn our [compost] heaps using the fork lift on the tractor') and weed-control. Unlike many twenty-first-century gardeners, Chatto was perfectly sanguine about using violently chemical weedkillers, painting them on to the leaves of offending vegetation with a small brush – an image I rather like. Less appealing is her use of peat to help retain moisture. Public knowledge about the loss of peat bogs was still limited in the late 1970s, but you'd have hoped that, as the partner of a bota-nist, she'd have been more habitat-aware.

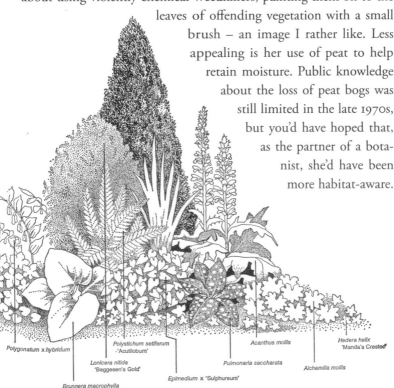

Polygonatum x hybridum

Polystichum setiferum ·'Acutilobum'

Acanthus mollis

Hedera helix 'Manda's Crested'

Lonicera nitida 'Baggesen's Gold'

Pulmonaria saccharata

Alchemilla mollis

Epimedium x 'Sulphureum'

Brunnera macrophylla

After some design basics ('hedges are a waste in the small dry garden') we finally get to the really good stuff: plants, and how she uses them. This is where you see how creative Chatto was, and how influential. Don't be surprised if, reading *The Dry Garden* now, you stumble across planting combinations that seem familiar. She describes filling the lowest layer of an oval island bed with dark green and cream crowns of *Helleborus argutifolius*, the fat, florid leaves of a purple bergenia, and spikes of the silver, grey and purple honesty *Lunaria annua* 'Variegata'. I'd put good money on at least one of the show gardens at the next Chelsea Flower Show mixing the loose, self-seeding wildness of annuals like honesty with architectural foliage plants like hellebores or bergenias. Elsewhere, in the difficult, dry shade of the kind you get beneath a large deciduous tree, she suggests pairing the airy, elegant fern *Dryopteris felix-mas* with white foxgloves and groundcover ivy, interspersed with tufts of Bowles' Golden Grass which, she says, look in spring like 'patches of sunlight dropped through the leafless branches'. You can still see examples of this restrained, all-about-the-foliage style in the narrow, shady gardens of London townhouses.

Those patches of dropping sunlight, though beautiful, are less typical. Don mentions that, on his first proper meeting with Chatto, she rather criticized his writing. That seems a case of the pot calling the Ming vase black. He is the most limpid of writers, probably better at communicating and evoking than he is at actual gardening. In a battle of horticulturalists, Chatto would be a world champion; but if the judges were scoring based on the poetry of her phrasing, she'd be out in round one.

She's still a pleasure to read, though, and not just because of the breadth of her knowledge. Chatto is one of those writers whose voice is so clear they could be standing next to you: slightly sharp, a tad bossy, never afraid to celebrate her successes, but equally unafraid of admitting mistakes. She's no John Lewis-Stempel or Robert Macfarlane, either of whom can turn a bug on a leaf into a universe, but she still makes you *see* things, mostly by helping you understand them. This is her on *Euphorbia characias subsp. wulfenii*, a Chatto favourite:

> In February the flower spike proudly lifts its bent head and gradually opens its massed lime-yellow florets into a huge cylindrical dome . . . Although they will stand cold, they grow skinny if whirled around by tearing winds. The protection of other shrubs is enough to make them wax fat.

Just try, next time you pass an *E. characias*, seeing its chubby, glaucous leaves without thinking of the phrase 'wax fat'.

The second half of the book initially looks as dry as a garden in August. It's nothing more than an alphabetical list of plants, conversational in tone, but mostly concerned with the detail of where plants originated from, what they look like, and where you might grow them. For a gardener, though, this holds exactly the same pleasures as cooks get from recipes, or decorators from fabric samples: the chance to dream. The plants may not be illustrated, but Chatto's words do a good enough job for the reader to indulge in some serious mind's-eye gardening. Will the 'great sheaves of shining evergreen leaves' of *Iris foetidissima var. citrina* look good spearing through the 'brassy yellow-edged' lemon balm, *Melissa officinalis* 'Aurea'? Dare you mix the floral, 'butterfly charm' of *Cistus* 'Silver Pink' with the 'huge, waving, sea-blue and waxen' foliage of *Crambe maritima*?

Dare away. And while you do, look forward to a long, hot and very, very dry summer.

ISABEL LLOYD is co-author of *Gardening for the Zombie Apocalypse: How to Grow Your Own Food When Civilization Collapses (or Even If It Doesn't)*, published last year. She lives in London and Sussex and manages to kill plants in both places.

Choppy Waters

MELISSA HARRISON

Dishonest or 'crooked' arguments are nothing new, but recently our fractious politics coupled with the invention of the Internet have lent them a fresh intensity, and a wider reach. Would that *Straight and Crooked Thinking*, written by Robert H. Thouless and first published in 1930, was now more widely read and taught in schools. This little book would not solve all our problems, of course, but it might help us see through partisan propaganda, take on unprincipled Internet warriors, persuade others honourably, defend our own beliefs effectively and (crucially) change our minds when necessary.

Part guide to rhetoric, part logic primer, *Straight and Crooked Thinking* was written in plain language for a general readership and produced with the support of the Workers' Educational Association – one of many clues to the author's own political leanings. Born in 1894, Robert Henry Thouless became a Fellow of Corpus Christi, Cambridge, went on to become Head of the Department of Psychology at Glasgow University, and then returned to Cambridge as a Reader. He died in 1984.

A devotee of the then revolutionary teachings of Sigmund Freud, Thouless was an idealist, as well as an evangelist for clear, logical thinking. He believed that a scientific approach to the public conversation around politics and economics would usher in a golden age of rationality, prosperity and accord between nations. 'We can solve the problems of war and poverty if we approach them in the same scientific spirit as we have now learned to apply to disease,' he writes. 'A

Robert H. Thouless, *Straight and Crooked Thinking* (1930)
Hodder & Stoughton · Pb · 192pp · £10.99 · ISBN 9781444117189

really educated democracy, distrustful of emotional phraseology and all the rest of the stock-in-trade of the exploiters of crooked thinking, devoid of reverence for ancient institutions and ancient ways of thinking, could take conscious control of our social development and could destroy these plagues of our civilization – war, poverty and crime . . . but the revolution must start in our own minds.'

Thouless begins by focusing on the use of emotionally toned words and introduces us to thirty-four 'dishonest tricks which are commonly used in argument, with the methods of overcoming them'. Some are probably common knowledge, albeit often only partially understood (for instance 'begging the question', an expression almost uniformly misrepresented these days); some, like 'the use of a syllogism with undistributed middle term', will probably be familiar to those whose education included a grounding in logic. But many will, I suspect, be new to the majority of modern readers, or understood only subconsciously.

So we learn to be alert for suggestion by prestige; for the recommendation of a position which is the mean between two extremes; for diversion by irrelevant objection; for proof by selected instances; for statements in which 'all' is implied but only 'some' is true (particularly rife on the Internet); for extension or misrepresentation of an opponent's position; for appeal to mere authority; for tabloid thinking (in its original sense of something made smaller, less complex and easy to swallow, like a tablet); for argument by imperfect analogy (also rife on the Internet); for special pleading, and many more. And as well as learning to identify these 'crooked' arguments when used by politicians, hucksters, professional controversialists, campaigners, journalists and our fellow civilians, Thouless challenges us to expunge them from our own arsenal – a far more arduous task.

Unsurprisingly, war casts a long shadow over the book – as do many other matters of the day. 'Wherever it is possible . . . I have made my illustrations from living controversial issues and from arguments that are actually used in defence of them,' Thouless states in his introduction. And so through the pages flicker the ghostly flames of debates that once burned as bright as those of today, many of which (but not all) have since lost their heat: the value of the League of Nations, the condition of the working man in Russia, disarmament treaties, 'agitators' in India, anti-Catholic prejudice, public versus private ownership, nativism, taxation, attitudes to same-sex relationships and racial inequality. This first edition was very much of its time, so it is no surprise that a few of Thouless's statements are likely to make the modern reader wince. Nevertheless, he was remarkably forward thinking on social issues, and his explicit aim was to equip readers with the tools to think logically about these very questions, particularly by examining their own beliefs and biases.

One of the most appealing things about *Straight and Crooked Thinking* is its repeated insistence that the goal of clear thinking and honest argument is not to help one score points or win a victory, but to discover the truth. To that end, what Thouless requires from us is humility in conflict of a kind that's rarely found, certainly not on social media and particularly not when it comes to those matters about which we feel strongly – the very matters concerning which he counsels us to be most on our guard against prejudice and fixity of thought. So when describing how to deal with the defence of an extreme position using the common formula 'The exception proves the rule', he first points out that in fact 'prove' once meant 'test', but then advises us that 'If one is anxious to discover the truth and not to triumph over one's opponent, one may try to discover what more moderate proposition is true.'

My 1945 edition has only one annotation by its original owner: in a section recommending that we put forward honestly the reasons we have for a belief, Thouless admits that such a method is likely to be unpopular with those 'who want a feeling of certainty rather than a knowledge of truth'. These words have been firmly underlined, and they struck me with just as much force as they clearly had the book's original owner – for who isn't tempted to linger in the safe harbour of conviction rather than venture out into the unsettlingly choppy waters of inquiry and doubt?

I've found only one bit of knavery in common use today that didn't find its way into Thouless's pages, for the simple reason that it would, I think, have been unconscionable in his day: that of taking up a position which requires that one appear stupid (despite being highly educated, and doubtless having a full grasp of the complexity of a situation) in order to appeal to those inclined to take a simplistic, black-and-white view. We might write this off as mere populism, which certainly existed in the 1930s, but I fear it now comes with a distinctly modern flavour: today's politicians know better than most that our old respect for expertise and education is at an all-time low.

Straight and Crooked Thinking is a book that really can change an open-minded reader for the better, in terms of behaviour in disputes, grasp of complex or prejudicially reported issues, and knowledge of the biases that risk marring our perception or narrowing our sympathies. But be warned: it's also a book that can make one even crosser with our flawed and fractious polity by bringing dirty tricks, lazy arguments and crooked thinking more clearly into view.

Strangely enough, Professor Thouless's admirably rational mind was no proof against beliefs we might now find a little surprising. He had a lifelong interest in the paranormal, conducted many experiments in parapsychology and wrote widely on ESP and psychokinesis. Indeed his belief that the dead could communicate with the living led him to leave behind a coded message in the hope that after his death, a medium could contact him to receive the key and thus crack the cipher. An award of $1,000 was offered, but no messages from the afterlife were received. Who knows, though: perhaps he had a look to see if his pleas for straight thinking and honest argument had caught on and transformed society, and decided that things being what they were, he was better off in the next place after all.

MELISSA HARRISON's latest novel, *All Among the Barley*, is set in the 1930s.

Dog's-eye View

REBECCA WILLIS

Last summer, something happened that showed me how utterly our lives are steeped in anthropomorphism. We got a dog. And she couldn't talk. Well, that's the shorthand version. The full text is that I'd caved in to over a decade of my children's pleading, we'd acquired a puppy, and I found that I didn't know how to relate to her or begin to understand her. Although she was clearly a beautiful creature, I wondered why on earth I'd taken on more responsibility when the freedom of an empty nest was just around the corner. I was regretting the whole enterprise when my sister happened to say that the puppy seemed kind. In a flash my feelings changed. 'Kind Dog!' I almost yelped. 'Like Kind Dog in the Ant and Bee books!' I felt a sudden rush of warmth and affection for this small creature which was now related to a fictional dog I'd loved as a child.

In case you weren't raised on them, the Ant and Bee books were an endearing, lightly educational series for children written in the 1950s and '60s by Angela Banner, in which Kind Dog helps the two insects out of various scrapes. Without really noticing, in the course of the story you learned about something: the alphabet, counting, colours. Kind Dog always wore a dark green hat, which our puppy didn't, but otherwise she did look a bit like him.

My Kind Dog moment shows how we project human emotions on to animals and how children's literature builds on that, as well as how long the effects of that literature endure. Our childhoods are

Alexandra Horowitz, *Inside of a Dog: What Dogs See, Smell and Know* (2009)
Simon & Schuster · Pb · 368pp · £8.99 · ISBN 9781849835671

peopled (significant word) by animals with human characteristics: Babar the Elephant, Beatrix Potter's tales, *The Wind in the Willows*, *The Jungle Book*, *Black Beauty*, *Watership Down*. There are good reasons for this. Using animals as people gives emotional distance when the message is powerful or scary or painful. It's also imaginative and fun and outside the rules that govern real life.

Once you start playing spot-the-talking-animal, you realize they're everywhere, not least on television where adverts are full of loquacious bulldogs and chirpy meerkats. Even the Bible has a chatty serpent in the first book and (less famously) a talking donkey in the Book of Numbers. Chaucer's Parliament of Fowls is a example of anthropomorphism used for social commentary – a rich tradition which continues right up to the work of one of my favourite cartoonists, Art Spiegelman. His profoundly moving graphic novel about the Holocaust, *Maus*, would almost certainly have been too much to bear if the Nazis and the Jews had been depicted as people rather than cats and mice: it's the same distancing principle as with the children's books.

Anthropomorphism is an innate part of our psychology: we have evolved to read each other's faces and we instinctively try to do the same with animals. It's seen in primitive religions – the Ancient Egyptians worshipped animals – and early myths and fables, such as Aesop's. But it doesn't equip you for owning a dog. Quite the contrary, in fact. For that you need another sort of book, and I don't mean the canine equivalent of those bringing-up-baby manuals, although there are plenty of them too. The book I discovered I needed as an antidote to my anthropomorphic upbringing is called *Inside of a Dog: What Dogs See, Smell and Know* (2009). It looks at what scientists know about the biology and psychology of dogs, and from that information tries to work out how the world seems to them.

Inside of a Dog was in the *New York Times* bestseller list for over a year and completely passed me by because, like the baby books, you don't need it until you've got your own. The author, Alexandra Horowitz, is uniquely qualified for the ambitious task of getting inside the bodies and minds of another species. Her CV includes a BA in philosophy and a PhD in cognitive science studying dogs, plus earlier stints as a lexicographer at Merriam-Webster and a fact-checker for the *New Yorker*. And, it perhaps goes without saying, she's a dog person: in the Acknowledgements section at the end of the book, the dogs come first.

Horowitz tells us not just what is known but how it is known, walking us through the various experiments that have been used in researching canine cognition in a way that is thorough but doesn't frighten the non-scientist. Where there is no reliable information on dogs, she describes studies of other animals that might shed some light. The content is scholarly but the execution is readable.

The first part of the book considers the physical ways in which the dog perceives the world. Most of us know that smell is the dog's dominant sense, the equivalent of sight for us, but here we find vivid details. A dog can detect a teaspoon of sugar in two Olympic-sized pools of water. A bloodhound has 600 million sensory receptor sites in its nose compared to our 6 million. Dogs have the weirdly named vomeronasal organ which sits about the roof of the mouth and turbo-charges their sense of smell. A scent gives them information about time, too – they can tell how long ago it was made. All of this means that the local lamp post is like a community noticeboard for a passing dog.

When it comes to sight, it's a myth that dogs see in black-and-white. Whereas humans have three kinds of photoreceptors (cones) on their retinae, dogs only have two, and fewer of them. The ones they lack are sensitive to red, so they experience colour most strongly when it's in the blue-green range. If we choose a red ball for our dog, it's to help us find it, not them. The arrangement of their retinal cells also means that they can't see things that are under their noses or focus as sharply as we do on things directly before them. Dogs with long noses have a 'visual streak' with the photoreceptors arranged more densely in a horizontal band across the middle of the eye, which gives them better panoramic and peripheral vision than humans –

useful for spotting prey. Dogs also have a higher 'flicker-fusion' rate than we do: if they see an old-style film they can spot the gaps between the frames. Because they see things a split second before we do, Horowitz suggests that to dogs we must always seem a little slow.

However, the book is far more than a series of not-many-people-know-that facts, fascinating though they are. The author is constantly trying, by using science 'rigorously, but creatively', to imagine what the dog's experience of the world – its so-called *Umwelt* – is like. And the thing that she keeps returning to is the extent to which their world is inextricably wrapped around ours. They are attuned to us in a way that feels magical, almost psychic – they seem to read us as if they have a sixth sense. This, she explains, is because 'through the artificial selection of domestication, they have evolved to be sensitive to just those things that importantly make up our cognition, including, critically, attention to others'. We may be studying them now, but they have been studying us for millennia: reading this book is just returning the compliment.

The second part of the book addresses dog cognition – what do they think about? What do they know? Do they have an awareness of the consciousness of another? It tackles their sense of time, of past and future, their sense of self (dogs routinely fail the mirror test, the standard test of animal self-awareness – but the author can't help pointing out that mirrors don't smell and maybe dogs don't care about appearances). It also asks whether they have a sense of mortality or of right and wrong. And it's bad news for people who think their dog is a person in disguise: that 'guilty' look is almost certainly a response to our body language and, despite anecdotal accounts of dogs rescuing people, experiments have shown that they don't recognize an emergency situation.

Yet our bond with dogs is so close that – apart from chimpanzees – they are the only species for which human yawning is contagious. The book ends by exploring this bond, which Horowitz breaks down into three parts – touch, the greeting ritual and timing. In the last of these she likens playing with a dog to a dance in which we match and mimic each other. Dogs are also good for our health, and not just because they force us to go on walks. When we're with them our feel-good hormones go up and our stress hormone, cortisol, goes down. It's mutual: human company can lower a dog's cortisol level, too.

The book's title plays on this quotation, attributed to Groucho Marx: 'Outside of a dog, a book is man's best friend. Inside of a dog, it's too dark to read.' It works better in American English, where 'outside of' means 'except for'. So we may miss the implied levity, the suggestion that the book captures the fun and joy of having a dog, and has a lighter touch than all the science might imply. To that end, the text is leavened with lyrical descriptions of the behaviour of Horowitz's adored dog, Pump (short for Pumpernickel). I wasn't sure about these sections at first – they seemed at odds with the scientific rigour and slightly gauche – but by the end I was so moved I had to wipe the tears from my eyes. These little hymns of appreciation remind us that science, love and a dash of anthropomorphism can co-exist.

As I look at our dog, now a sleek, mostly obliging one-year-old, I feel a debt of gratitude to this book. It provides a much-needed counterbalance to the anthropomorphism that is all around us. Of course I think I can tell what she's feeling behind those big, amber eyes, and sometimes I do still wish she could speak. But at the same time I'm very aware of how she might perceive the world and how our actions and demands might seem to her. If Kind Dog helped me to love her, *Inside of a Dog* helped me to understand and respect her. It gave her the dignity and separateness that she deserves. It made me love her not for her similarity to me but for her otherness. For her creatureness. For her dogness.

In the days when she was absolutely, categorically, never ever going to own a dog, REBECCA WILLIS was Travel Editor of *Vogue* and Associate Editor of *Intelligent Life*.

The dogs in this article were drawn by Gavin Maxwell, Gwen Raverat and Richard Kennedy.

A Frank Look at History

ANDY MERRILLS

I am a book annotator. Of course I never write in the margins of library books, and I wouldn't dream of marking books lent by a well-meaning friend: I'm a book annotator, not a sociopath. But a pencilled note or punctuation mark in the margin of my own books is a form of ownership, a tiny graphite beacon for future browsing and (on occasion) an aid to concentration. Most of these notes are unobtrusive – a line here, an asterisk there – but there is one book that I own which is annotated to the point of deranged excess: the Penguin Classic by Gregory of Tours, entitled *The History of the Franks* and translated by Lewis Thorpe. Its 700 pages are covered in pencilled comments and cross-references and notes in blue, black and green biro, its cover cross-hatched by the tiny wrinkles and folds that only a well-loved paperback can have. It is probably the one book I would save if my house caught fire, and not simply because Gregory describes a lot of burning houses.

There are two reasons for the surfeit of annotation in my copy. The first (and most obvious) is that Gregory's *History* was a core text in my undergraduate degree and was pored over with a diligence that approached frenzy when Finals loomed. The second reason is that Gregory's is both a complex text and an exceptionally rich one – this is the work of a historian who had a thousand things to say, who recounted triumphs and disasters, and described them in tangential passages about blood-feuds and curses. It is a book to be read with

Gregory of Tours, *The History of the Franks* (6th century AD) · Trans. Lewis Thorpe
Penguin · Pb · 720pp · £14.99 · ISBN 9780140442953

fingers in a dozen pages at once. Or by writing in the margins in biro.

Gregory was bishop of the French city of Tours in the latter half of the sixth century AD. At the time, most of what is now France (and parts of Germany and the Low Countries) was ruled by the Merovingian dynasty of the Franks, who established their kingdoms in the shell of the Roman Gallic provinces. The most famous Merovingian was King Clovis, who was said to have been the grandson of a sea-monster. He converted his people to Catholic Christianity and had a nasty habit of decapitating disrespectful underlings with lusty blows of his axe. Clovis had been dead for around eighty years at the time when Gregory was writing, but he continued to cast a long shadow over the world he had created. In Gregory's time, Frankia was ruled by Clovis's sons and grandsons – the 'long-haired kings' of later French foundation myths – who jostled for influence and sought to expand their power over these rich lands and over one another.

But for all their violent internecine squabbling, this was not a wholly 'barbaric' society. As Bishop of Tours, Gregory had an important status within this early medieval world: he was a representative of a new episcopal aristocracy who took on much of the burden of civil leadership, and who helped maintain classical culture in a period we traditionally regard as a 'dark age'. Gregory himself came from a prominent family and enjoyed his own close network of alliances and friendships across Gaul. As a result, *The History* charts the collision of different cultures and represents the attempts of one man to make sense of – and perhaps shape – this changing world. It is this which makes the work so endlessly rewarding to modern readers.

Lewis Thorpe's Penguin translation is the most easily accessible English rendering of the text. As a translation it is far from perfect – Gregory's intended title was actually *The Ten Books of Histories* (or simply *Histories*) – and on top of this there are some strange renderings of the Latin, and some frankly bizarre footnotes, which reveal some of Thorpe's less progressive political attitudes. But ease of availability can make up for a lot, and the translation certainly makes for a gripping read. What the Penguin version doesn't provide, however (and what no edition should), is the crucial advice to the first-time reader: don't start at the beginning. Instead, read the preface and then skip ahead to Book 3, where the real action starts. In doing so, you'll miss out Gregory's long preamble on Biblical history, the Roman Empire and the early bits of Frankish history down to the death of Clovis. These are worth coming back to eventually (especially the bits about Clovis), but the early parts are confusing for the unprepared reader, and slow-going compared with what comes later. Instead, nip forward to Book 3 and the reigns of Clovis's four warring sons, Theuderic, Chlodomer, Childebert and Lothar, and be plunged straight into the glorious early medieval world of bishops, nuns, saints and blood-feuds.

Thereafter, *The History* is a patchwork of vivid episodes which are a joy to read even if the precise significance of what is happening can sometimes be hard to follow. As befits a history which covers several generations and a large swathe of western Europe, the text is stuffed with hundreds of characters, many with appealingly strange (or frustratingly similar) names. Some of the more prominent become familiar friends as the work progresses – the scheming King Chilperic, who had pretensions to literary sophistication but could only sign his name by using a stencil; the pious King Guntram, who donated relics to Gregory's church at Tours but ordered horse dung to be flung at diplomats who displeased him; and of course Gregory himself – always measured, always just, always seeming to hide something. Other figures appear less regularly, and move in and out of the narrative, as the action switches between kingdoms. But Gregory's succinct sketches populate this world with a rich tangle of distinct figures, even if they can sometimes be a little overwhelming in their profusion.

Some of the most memorable characters only appear once. Sichar and Chramnesind were two Frankish nobles known only from three paragraphs of Gregory's work, but who are emblematic of the text as a whole. After a night of heavy drinking, these two fast friends fell out, primarily because Sichar boasted excessively about having killed several close relatives of Chramnesind. Naturally, Chramnesind took this rather badly, responded in kind and so started a brutal conflict between the two families, triggering a diplomatic crisis between the kingdoms of Chilperic and Guntram. Things did not end well.

In a similar vein, Gregory tells us of two brothers called Salonius and Sagittarius, who probably came from an old Gallo-Roman family, to judge from their names. Both became bishops but, unlike Gregory, they used their influence for nefarious ends, establishing themselves as mobsters or petty gangsters in the region around Lyons, and avoided disgrace only through the misguided support of the Pope. This reprieve proved brief; Salonius and Sagittarius turned to feasting, alcohol and fornication, and were eventually thrown in prison. Gregory's account closes with the tantalizing note that they escaped but says nothing more about their fate.

This marvellous tableau is rich in female characters too: many of Gregory's greatest villains (and heroes) are women. The historian reserves particular bile for Queen Fredegund, the consort of King Chilperic, and regent for her son Chlothar II. (If you are starting to wonder about the names, you can begin to appreciate why my copy of the text is so heavily marked.) Fredegund is certainly the villain of Gregory's work and he catalogues her scheming and skulduggery, and her attempted assassination of at least five other Merovingian figures with fascinated horror. Yet in spite of this, she remains an impressive figure and somehow retains her glamorous dignity even when she is having a literal punch-up with her own daughter.

All of this may make Gregory's Frankia seem very bloody – and it certainly was – but the violence is tempered by a deep religiosity. On occasion this is the quiet faith which we might today associate with the monks and nuns of the early Church, and this was certainly a world of many saints. But these churchmen and women still lived within a bloody world, even when they weren't personally bashing heads. Gregory also describes a robust Christian world – of saints who cause the shackles to leap from the limbs of recalcitrant prisoners, or a God who causes sinful rulers to die in the most hideous and painful ways. Gregory's model bishop was not a churchman who piously intoned from the pulpit but one who got his hands dirty in the names of his parishioners and supplicants.

Perhaps more importantly, Gregory's is a profoundly human work, and often a very funny one. For a long time, the Bishop of Tours was regarded as a disingenuous commentator on the world around him: the helter-skelter nature of his *History* seemed so strange that it was hard to detect a literary or political plan behind it all, and the writer was simply assumed to have just written what he saw without much thought.

Modern commentators on the text (and there are many) are much less certain of this, and *The History* is now most commonly read as a deft attempt to navigate through the difficult environment of the sixth century: to create a place for the Church, for Gregory, for his favoured friends and relations, in this world, and to make sense of it too. But even this image of Gregory as literary architect cannot deny the power of his succinct personal sketches – of the evil queen or the stupid king, of the greedy monks who were drowned in a tsunami on Lake Geneva when digging for treasure, or the citizens of Poitiers who tried to steal St Martin's relics to glorify their own church. Gregory's *History* is fascinating for these details just as it remains a puzzle in the wider sense. I've been returning to it for years – and adding brief notes each time – and still don't really understand it. And that seems like a good recommendation to me.

ANDY MERRILLS once confessed his love of Gregory of Tours in a cover letter seeking archaeological work in France. This led to merciless teasing over the months that followed, but he stands by his opinion. He now writes and teaches on the early medieval world, especially North Africa.

Walden-by-the-Sea

RICHARD PLATT

It is a typical winter night on California's central coast: the rain has been drumming on the roof, the dogs, happy and dry, are curled up in their beds, and my wife and I are in our bed, propped up on a pile of pillows, books in hand. I'm attempting with mixed success not to shake the bed with repressed laughter brought on by P. G. Wodehouse. My wife, having put aside the ever-present *New Yorker* magazine, is giving her undivided attention to *The Outermost House* by Henry Beston.

'Darling, have you read this?' she says, her eyes remaining fixed on the page.

'Mm. Must be more than twenty years ago. It's very good.'

'It's better than "very good",' she replies. 'You should read it again. It's wonderful.'

The following night Mr Beston and I become reacquainted, and I am reminded why my wife was so insistent that he and I meet again.

In 1922, the 34-year-old Henry Beston Sheahan, having served as an ambulance driver in France in the First World War and as a war correspondent on both British and American naval ships, was looking for a quiet place; a place not 'harassed of man'. A native of Massachusetts, he chose the great beach at Cape Cod, a skeletal extension of land

Henry Beston, *The Outermost House* (1928)
Pushkin Press · Pb · 224pp · £9.99 · ISBN 9781911590149

thrusting thirty miles east from Massachusetts then curling northward, defying the wrath of the north Atlantic, like the flexed bicep of a body-builder shaking a heavily knuckled fist at Nova Scotia.

Beston's visits grew in length and duration, and in 1925 he purchased fifty acres on the beach at Eastham and built a two-room house, sixteen feet by twenty, with ten windows. Its living space was so open to the ocean vista that it felt like a ship at sea, and so close – twenty feet above the high-water mark and thirty from the beach – that his reading was interrupted one night by the thunderous impact of a massive wave that jarred the pictures hanging on the walls and sent a quiver through the flame of his oil lamp. He christened his house the Fo'castle.

Beston began keeping a journal of his observations, intending per-haps to shape them into a book, though it was slow in coming. When he met the woman to whom he would propose, the fellow-writer Elizabeth Coatsworth, his book was still only a sheaf of notes. It is said that Miss Coatsworth declined to marry him until his book was finished. This story is almost certainly apocryphal, but if it isn't true, it should be. For a man who stands within striking distance of his fortieth wedding anniversary, as I do, it has the ring of authenticity. The Bestons' marriage was to be a long one. One does not maintain a long and successful marriage without having learned The Art of Easy Acquiescence. *The Outermost House* was published in 1928. The Bestons married in 1929.

Unlike many writers who flee to the quiet seclusion of the country in search of themselves – the parallels with Thoreau are inescapable – Beston knows who he is and what he wants. He wants not to look inward but outward. He wants to be a spectator, and it is a fine spectacle he has chosen: the restless north Atlantic, predatory and unforgiving in its darker, wintry moods, benign and life-giving in the brief, steamy months of summer. Just steps away, the ocean offers him something beyond quiet; it offers him the rhythmic percussion of its relentless crash and the treble hiss of sand as the waters retreat. He has a wonderful ear, and the great beach of Cape Cod is his amphitheatre, where 'as the year lengthened into autumn, the beauty and mystery of this earth and outer sea so possessed and held me that I could not go', and as we walk the beach beside him we feel as if we, too, cannot go.

> The world today is sick to its thin blood for lack of elemental things, for fire before the hands, for water welling from the earth, for air, for the dear earth itself underfoot. In my world of beach and dune these elemental presences lived and had their being, and under their arch there moved an incomparable pageant of nature and the year. The flux and reflux of the ocean, the in-comings of waves, the gatherings of birds, the pilgrimages of the peoples of the sea, winter and storm, the splendour of autumn and the holiness of spring – all these were part of the great beach.

This is pure Thoreau, but while Beston is occasionally impelled to reflection, he is less a philosopher than a poet, for he believes that 'Poetry is as necessary to comprehension as science. It is as impossible to live without reverence as it is without joy.' Whether it is the tens of thousands of birds who visit the Cape, flowing across the sky like 'a river of life', the ever-changing moods of the sea (the birth and death of a single wave is the subject of an entire chapter), or the infinite shadings of the shifting sand beneath his feet, his artist's eye is ever alive to the colour and texture of everything around him.

Though first and foremost an observer and a poet, speculating on the habits of the many unseen creatures who leave their tracks in the sand or 'vanish into the trackless nowhere of the sky', he finds 'there is always reserve and mystery, always something beyond, on earth and sea something which nature, honouring, conceals', and his observations lead inevitably to moments of reflection.

> We need another and a wiser and perhaps a more mystical con-cept of animals ... We patronize them for their incompleteness, for their tragic fate of having taken form so far below ourselves.

And therein we err . . . For the animals shall not be measured by man. In a world older and more complete than ours they move finished and complete, gifted with extensions of the senses we have lost or never attained, living by voices we shall never hear . . . [they are] other nations, caught with ourselves in the net of life and time, fellow prisoners of the splendour and travail of the earth.

The Outermost House is now regarded as belonging on the short shelf that houses the indispensable books about Cape Cod, and visitors to the cape today may be seen traipsing about with it in hand, the shade of Henry Beston beside them, and running before them 'the thin-footed, light-winged peoples, the industrious waders, the busy pickup, runabout, and scurry-along folk'. Like Henry David Thoreau's beloved cabin at Walden Pond, the original outermost house, proclaimed a National Literary Landmark in 1964, is long gone. The Fo'castle and the beach on which it once stood were claimed by the sea in the catastrophic winter storms of 1977–8, but Beston's work and its legacy have achieved something like immortality.

An environmentalist before the label became fashionable, or even entered the vernacular, Henry Beston has opened the eyes of generations of writers and readers to the wonders of everything that can elevate man; that man cannot create but can imperil by neglect or indifference. A small, beautiful corner of the world is safer from exploitation because Henry Beston was there. *The Outermost House* helped to inspire the creation in 1961 of the 43,000-acre Cape Cod National Seashore, and Beston, who lived to see it, surely knew that this is as fine a monument to a man's life and work as anyone could wish for.

RICHARD PLATT lives quietly in a small, not-quite-outermost house near the sea, in the mist, wind and fog of California's central coast. He is the author of *Ripples from Walden Pond* and *As One Devil to Another*.

Prophesying War

PAUL BRASSLEY

I enjoy reading thrillers. I might like to claim that literary fiction is my constant companion, but for most of the time it isn't – the novels that Graham Greene described as his 'entertainments' give me far greater pleasure than his more serious books. Similarly, when my work as a historian took me to the period between the First and Second World Wars I found that Eric Ambler's thrillers, written at the time, effectively captured the contemporary atmosphere, just as do Alan Furst's more recent books. Both explore the impact of the interwar struggle between fascism, communism and democracy on innocent individuals, men who find their lives tossed about on the great waves of history. But always men. What about the women?

One of the books I read when beginning my own work on that period was *Europe of the Dictators* by Elizabeth Wiskemann, from which it was clear that her historical writing was informed by her own past. I wanted to know more, so I tracked down her autobiography, *The Europe I Saw* (1968). I was captivated. Here was a woman whose adventures in real life might have formed a model for the fictions of Greene, Ambler or Furst. But she was more than one of the little people whose fate was determined by big events and powerful people; she met many of the powerful, and she played her part in the big events.

The Europe I Saw is not a conventional autobiography, although from its first few pages we learn that Elizabeth Wiskemann was born in 1899, the youngest child of a mother with Welsh and Huguenot

---

Elizabeth Wiskemann, *The Europe I Saw* (1968), is out of print but we can obtain second-hand copies.

roots and a German father who had moved to London as a young man. She went to Newnham College, Cambridge, where she took a first-class degree in history in 1921. Several difficult and poverty-stricken years followed before she became a history tutor at Newnham, where she worked on her doctoral thesis.

For some reason she had attracted the enmity of her senior examiner, and her thesis on Napoleon III and the Roman Question was only awarded an M.Litt. As a result she left Cambridge and went to Berlin in the autumn of 1930: 'If I had remained an academic specializing in the nineteenth century, I suppose my life would have been considerably duller than it became.' After this introduction, the first half of the book is divided into chapters on each of the countries of central Europe during the ferment of the 1930s, as seen by a working journalist with the mind of a historian and a well-stocked address book.

Following her initial visit to Germany in the last years of the Weimar Republic she returned to Cambridge and by 1932 she had settled into a rhythm, 'teaching in Cambridge during the University term and spending a maximum vacation period in Germany or some area related to it in order to describe what was happening there'.

Her first article was sold to the *New Statesman* in April 1932, and thereafter she found that by writing four articles after each journey she could fund another few weeks abroad providing she lived frugally. She became a regular visitor to Germany, and also Austria, Czechoslovakia, Yugoslavia, Hungary, Romania and Poland. She had a talent for making contacts, not only in politics and journalism but also in the arts. She saw the original production of Brecht's *Threepenny Opera*, danced with the caricaturist and satirist George Grosz, spent an evening in a Vienna café with the philosopher György Lukács and the writer Robert Musil, and took tea with Thomas Mann and his family.

The first two chapters of the book, on Germany, vividly evoke the atmosphere of the time. Attending her first Nazi rally, she was filled with foreboding, and she subsequently witnessed Nazi violence at first hand. By 1933, when she returned to Berlin a few days after Hitler became Chancellor, she had acquired the habit of not mentioning names on the telephone or writing them in full in her diary. Her articles increasingly drew attention to the dangers of Nazism, and on 17 February 1936 the police in Munich, having taken exception to one of them, issued instructions that her arrival in Germany be officially reported.

When she returned to Berlin in July she was arrested and taken to the Gestapo's headquarters on Prinz Albrechtstrasse. There she was interrogated, rather ineffectively, about her articles, while British Embassy staff, alerted by Norman Ebbut, the *Times* correspondent whom she had been visiting when arrested, attempted to have her released. Her interrogator, 'the blond beast type' in full SS uniform, wanted her to admit to having written anti-German statements. Could she have stated that Jews were maltreated? 'I said why yes, it's true, isn't it?' After three hours she was told that if she signed a statement that she could have written such material, and in view of the forthcoming Olympic Games, she would be released. She signed, returned to Ebbut's flat, 'drank six strong drinks straight off' with no noticeable effect, and left the country the following day.

She could no longer return to Germany, but, as the following chapters reveal, she could still follow the impact of Nazi policy by visiting other countries in central Europe, and her talent for making contacts gave her access to some of the most prominent political figures of the time. For example, thanks to having met his son at a lunch in London, the first person she interviewed in Prague was Tómaš Masaryk, the President of Czechoslovakia. In Vienna, she spoke to Hitler's special envoy to Austria, Franz von Papen, the former German Chancellor; in Budapest to István Bethlen after he had ceased to be Prime Minister; in Romania to the leader of the Peasant Party; and in Warsaw to General Sikorski, future leader of the Polish government-in-exile. She also knew journalists from all over Europe. By 1939 she had written one book on the relationship between the Czechs and the Germans and another, on Europe post-Munich, which appeared in November 1939, inopportunely entitled *Undeclared War*.

By then she had decided that her most useful wartime role would be to work for the Foreign Office in Switzerland, where she had numerous foreign contacts. After an interview with a top security official, who told her that she was 'not nearly such a fool as he had expected a woman would be', she went to Zurich in January 1940. Part of her job, after Dunkirk, was to monitor the output of the German press, an operation which hitherto had been carried out in the Low Countries. She was also responsible for reporting on *Stimmung*, 'the German state of mind and everything contributing to it'. This required her to build contacts with anyone who had access to the country: Swiss Berlin correspondents visiting home, Swiss businessmen visiting Germany, and Germans visiting Switzerland. She was one of the few British diplomats who was allowed to meet enemy subjects, so she cultivated as many as she could find, from businessmen and theatrical people to Adam von Trott, the diplomat who was later hanged for plotting against Hitler. Her account of him demonstrates the strain that must have attended her daily life during the war:

> He caused me great anxiety. With his striking appearance – that immensely high forehead – he was someone you could not miss, and in those days only Poles or Germans were called Adam. So when he rang me up and said in his nearly perfect English 'It's Adam speaking' anyone listening in could be in no doubt that it was Adam von Trott zu Solz. I begged him to call himself Tom, Dick, or Harry – I was so trained to recognize voices by then that this would have caused me no difficulty. Yet he never could bring himself to take this simple precaution. He was a bewilderingly brilliant creature, infinitely German in the intellectual complexity in which he loved to indulge . . . [He] had a brother fighting in Russia and I tried to get him to tell me about *Stimmung* on the *Ostfront*; I seldom got anything but his own political theories.

I began to wonder if there was any supporting evidence for her stories. When I was working in the National Archives at Kew I typed 'Berne Legation', where she was based from 1940, into the online catalogue. I was rewarded by two fat Foreign Office files of intelligence reports. They demonstrated the variety of information she gathered: on food rationing in France, the impact of air raids, student riots in Munich, criticism of BBC broadcasts to the occupied countries, a warning of the forthcoming German attack on Yugoslavia in 1941, and rumours of a shortage of raw materials in Germany in 1942. They were mostly in typescript, but there were a few pages in her handwriting. When you have become fascinated by the life of a person you will never meet, holding a report actually written by them produces a wonderful sense of contact. And these files contained, in effect, the raw material for the second half of *The Europe I Saw*, so reading them was like peering over the author's shoulder as she wrote.

They show that she was not a spy in the sense that she operated under cover in enemy territory, but she was certainly a collector of intelligence, and she had to be careful about the security of her material and not draw attention to those she met. As she tells us, among them were several art dealers, who were invaluable because, like actors, they had international connections. They included the Wertheimers, husband and wife, German Jews who had escaped to Paris and then from Vichy France to Basle. They gave her a drawing by Piranesi, 'as a prize for helping the Jews', they said. She valued it above any wartime decoration: 'It is the focus of my sitting-room today and is destined for the Fitzwilliam museum.'

What happened to it, I wondered? I went to the online catalogue. Object number PD.44-1971 in the Fitzwilliam Museum in Cambridge is a small drawing of a seated figure, in brown ink on paper, and measuring about five inches by two and a half, by the Italian eighteenth-century architect and artist Giovanni Battista Piranesi. The accompanying note on its provenance states that it was 'Presented to Miss Elizabeth Wiskemann by representatives of the art trade in gratitude for her courageous and tireless efforts on behalf of refugees during World War II'.

The Piranesi drawing
© The Fitzwilliam Museum,
Cambridge

Elizabeth Wiskemann continued to work as a journalist and writer after the war, but increasingly she returned to her original career as an academic historian, with teaching posts at Edinburgh and Sussex, and several important books to her name. She was, according to those who knew her, a small vivacious woman of great charm and independence. Sadly, by the early 1970s her eyesight was failing. Rather than face a future in which she would be unable to read, in July 1971 she took her own life. It was a life that in the 1930s and '40s might have sprung from the imagination of a thriller writer, but for which we have the written evidence that it actually happened.

PAUL BRASSLEY lives on Dartmoor, and although no longer paid to do so, continues to work as a historian.

Jeremy's Progress

HELEN MACEWAN

My grandparents' books were ranged in a deep alcove by the fireplace, a shadowy and mysterious recess that invited exploration. During visits in school holidays, I read my way through those faded hardbacks and ever afterwards associated their authors with the thrill of exploring that dark corner. The pleasurably fusty smell of the pages seemed to me the smell of an epoch, of the generation of my grandparents, born in the 1890s. Over the years I made the acquaintance of the writers they had grown up with – Galsworthy, Arnold Bennett, Hugh Walpole.

Ah, Hugh Walpole. Who reads him now? So prolific (36 novels by the time he died in 1941, still in his fifties), so well-loved in his day. He didn't always find favour with highbrow critics; a traditionalist in an age of experimentation, a romantic in an age of realism, he broke no moulds – but his books were bestsellers and his reputation stood high, at least before Somerset Maugham lampooned him in *Cakes and Ale* as the talentless, tirelessly networking Alroy Kear. The postwar world appears to have endorsed Maugham's verdict; at any rate, although Walpole's Herries saga has found fans, he has been largely discarded as old-fashioned and irrelevant. And yet of all the books in that alcove it was a slim volume of Walpole's, a favourite of my mother's before me, that I loved and which I appropriated and took home with me: *Jeremy* (1918), the first in his trilogy about a young boy.

I doubt that Walpole himself would have picked this out as the

---

Hugh Walpole, *Jeremy* (1918), *Jeremy and Hamlet* (1923) and *Jeremy at Crale* (1927) are out of print but we can obtain second-hand copies.

work for which he most deserves to be remembered. It was hugely popular at the time, as attested by the number of boys named after its eponymous hero in the years following its publication, but he put far more labour and ambition into other novels (*Jeremy* was written in spare moments while Walpole was doing propaganda work in Russia during the First World War). Yet while whatever else of his I read in youth has long faded from my memory, *Jeremy* has stayed with me, one of those books that make themselves comfortably at home in your imagination and never leave.

It charts ten months in the life of 8-year-old Jeremy Cole, in the small cathedral town of Polchester in Glebeshire, before he is packed off to boarding school – the last months of the innocence of early childhood. No one knew better than Walpole did, from painful experience, the loss of innocence once a boy is submerged in school life. The second novel in the series, *Jeremy and Hamlet* (1923), switches between school and home, with Jeremy having to readjust to home life in the holidays with the help of his boon companion, his dog Hamlet – an important character in his own right. In the last, *Jeremy at Crale* (1927), Jeremy is 15 and all the action takes place at his public school.

At the start of the first and, for me, most engaging of the novels (though all three are full of excellent things), which opens on Jeremy's eighth birthday, his universe is still largely that of the nursery, shared with sisters Mary and Helen and ruled over by their nurse, nick-named the Jampot. The children's mother is a placid presence in the background, their clergyman father, unimaginative and ineffectual, mostly a non-presence. Two other members of the household loom large: silly, interfering Aunt Amy, who always rubs the children up the wrong way, and Uncle Samuel, sarcastic and inscrutable, an unsuccessful painter who's the black sheep of the family. Jeremy knows that, of all his circle, it is Uncle Samuel who understands him best, but he's generally invisible in his studio – except when he disappears to 'that mysterious, unseen, unfathomed country, Paris'.

From the opening chapters, Jeremy's horizons are already starting to widen beyond the nursery. The departure of the Jampot and the arrival of Hamlet, henceforth his companion in adventure, are early milestones in his growing quest for independence. It is a quest which naturally brings conflict with uncomprehending adults, who view as disobedience what is only the assertion of his individuality, the expansion of his spirit. The theme of the novel and of the trilogy as a whole is 'Jeremy's progress', with each episode marking a 'station'.

Jeremy is the first of Walpole's Polchester books. Subsequently the setting for *The Old Ladies* and other novels, this fictional city was chiefly inspired by his mother's home town of Truro, though for its cathedral he drew on Durham, where he went to school. Polchester became so real to Walpole's readers that an American fan mapped it out and drew it in loving detail, and in *Jeremy* it is vividly introduced through the eyes of a child for whom everything in it is an object of wonder and enjoyment.

On the face of it, the world of Polchester is familiar from countless other chronicles of Edwardian and late Victorian childhoods (both Jeremy and Walpole were born in 1884): a world of teas and curates and governesses, unmarried aunts and uncles, and phalanxes of servants. *Jeremy* was written during the Great War, so it is inevitable that it conveys a feeling of nostalgia for a lost golden age.

Childhood *per se*, however, is by no means viewed as a golden period. It wasn't a happy time for Walpole himself. Bullied at school, he was in some ways unlike his sturdily independent hero and, as he points out in the preface, the novel is not straightforwardly autobiographical. As a child Walpole had more in common with Jeremy's sister Mary, the 'clever' one of the siblings, who takes refuge from a bruising world in the novels of Charlotte Mary Yonge and endless romances of her own invention. With her stringy hair and huge spectacles, hypersensitivity and inconvenient hunger for appreciation and affection ('You *do* love me, Jeremy, don't you?'), the ever-suffering Mary furnishes some moving passages.

Like George Eliot in her account of the early trials of Maggie Tulliver, Walpole knew that, as he tells us in *Jeremy at Crale*, 'the catastrophes of childhood are eternal'. When Jeremy is denied a much-anticipated trip to a pantomime as punishment for a minor misdemeanour, his universe plunges into a darkness that seems final. 'His whole world was gone.' Delivered from despair by Uncle Samuel and smuggled into the show, his rapture is as intense as his previous misery. What Jeremy does have in common with Walpole, apart from sensitivity and imagination, is a sense of wonder and a capacity for enjoyment. The landmarks that punctuate his year – the Christmas pantomime, the annual holiday at Cow Farm on the Glebeshire coast, the autumn fair, disapproved of by his parents as a magnet for undesirables and declared out of bounds – are for him objects of passionate surmise and expectation, experiences his expanding spirit craves.

To Jeremy, *Dick Whittington* at the Polchester Assembly Rooms, with their smell of gas and oranges, is, quite literally, magic. His merry-go-round ride on a black 'steed' during an unauthorized visit to the fair whirls him far away from the sphere of the nursery and the rocking-horse into an intoxicating exaltation and feeling of power. 'He had long known that this glory was somewhere if it could only be found, all his days he seemed to have been searching for it.'

Walpole unpicks the complexities of the emotions felt even at moments of ecstasy like these. On arrival at Cow Farm at the start of the holidays Jeremy detects, at the heart of his almost intolerable happiness, 'a strange unhappiness that he had never known before' born of growing awareness of his separateness from the rest of the family. Experience can never be fully shared; he's 'caught into a life that was utterly his own'.

There are many such moments of insight, and of darkness and strangeness. Jeremy has intimations of 'a world adjacent to this one' on the sands of Rafiel Cove, said to be haunted by the Scarlet Admiral of local legend, seen landing one summer morning from a splendid ship to fight a duel to the death on the cliffs. In *Jeremy and Hamlet*, venturing alone into the cathedral, he has a vision of the gauntleted Black Bishop who lies buried beneath its flags, another figure of local legend who fought to the death. He senses a past that is as real as the present, a past that *is* the present.

And there is the mounting horror of a day on which his mother hangs between life and death, and his gradual conviction that the Old Testament God of his father's morning sermon demands a sacrifice in return for her life – and that the sacrifice required is Hamlet, his closest friend. The sudden blackening of the sky as he wrestles with this idea, a clap of thunder and Hamlet's abrupt disappearance as a storm breaks bring a revelation as well as terror: 'In that moment he believed in God.'

At certain points in his 'progress', the mysterious forces he encounters are forces of darkness within himself. In tormenting Miss Jones, the elderly governess who replaces the Jampot, he finds in himself a new power and capacity for cruelty.

> It was something indecent, sinister, secret, foreign to his whole nature felt by him now for the first time, unanalysed, of course, but belonging, had he known it, to that world of which afterwards he was often to catch glimpses, that world of shining white faces in dark streets, of muffled cries from shuttered windows, of muttered exclamations, half caught, half understood. He was never again to be quite free from the neighbourhood of that half-world; he would never be quite sure of his dominance of it until he died.

In a disturbing episode, Jeremy's long-standing dream of running away to sea turns to obsession when a sailor grants him a sight of his tattoos. When he is stalked by the man for weeks after this encounter, pleasure mingles with fear. 'Strangest of all was the sense of evil that came with the attraction.' The seafarer's own interest, as it turns out, is not in Jeremy himself but in the contents of the Coles' house.

Even so, the emotions explored, like those at play in the game of 'teasing Miss Jones', are murky.

Jeremy is a book *about* children, therefore, rather than *for* children. In the course of it, he grows in empathy as well as self-knowledge, becoming increasingly aware of the adults around him as people in their own right and not just the backdrop to his own drama. When he finds Miss Jones in tears and learns her history, she springs to life as a real, suffering person. 'The world seemed to be suddenly filled with pressing, thronging figures, all with businesses of their own.' Perhaps, he realizes, even Aunt Amy has a history, and cries.

Most intriguing and enigmatic of all the adults is Uncle Samuel, untidy and unshaven, with his paint-stained smock, crimson slippers, blue tam-o'-shanter and cryptic remarks. He is not yet the mentor and confidant he becomes later in the trilogy, when Jeremy is admitted to the sanctum of the studio. Even at 8, though, Jeremy senses that this disreputable relative has more to teach him than the other adults of the family; only Uncle Samuel, like Jeremy himself, views things through the eyes of the imagination.

In Walpole's books about adult passions we are conscious of his limitations. Entertaining and gripping at his best, at his worst he can appear shallow and facile. But in articulating a child's feelings he is masterly. *Jeremy* resonates with the sense of mystery and wonder, of being a child in a world that is both frightening and marvellous.

HELEN MACEWAN is a translator. She is also the author of books about Charlotte Brontë's time in Brussels, which has been her home for the past fifteen years, and of a life of Winifred Gérin, a Brontë biographer with a Belgian link.

Time for Rhyme

CLARE MORRALL

There's a picture in *The Third Ladybird Book of Nursery Rhymes* of a small, nervous boy in knickerbockers appearing before a man of authority: 'I do not like thee, Doctor Fell,/ The reason why, I cannot tell./ But this I know and know full well,/ I do not like thee, Doctor Fell.' It's a curious little thing, but somehow very pleasing. It rhymes, there's a clear, easy rhythm behind the words and we're familiar with the sentiment. In short, it's a typical nursery rhyme.

I became interested in nursery rhymes when I was writing my last novel, *When the Floods Came*. The novel is set in the near future and I wanted a heritage for the children, something that would connect them – living in an otherwise empty tower block and surrounded by a crumbling, watery world – to their parents' old life. A book of nursery rhymes provided the solution, with the words and pictures embedded in everyone's memory, little gems of harmless nonsense that are reminders of the past, that link people from all ages and backgrounds. So I unearthed the three *Ladybird Books of Nursery Rhymes* that I'd read to my children. They were surprisingly familiar, almost as if they came from my own childhood, but the dates of publication – 1965, 1966, 1967 – make it clear that they didn't. How interesting that they've remained with me for decades when they're not mine at all. Now that I have rediscovered them, though, it worries me that they're losing their place in our collective memory, marching down the hill with the Grand Old Duke of York and lacking the energy to march back up again. Do they still have a place alongside the electronic entertainment of today's children?

But when I open them there's something wrong. Some of the

words that I remember are different from the ones in the books. How can this be? You've got it wrong, I want to say. My version is the only right one. Obviously! Could this be the result of regional pronunciation, perhaps, a change in emphasis? No, geography can't alter rhythm. I imagine an editor making alterations, missing the point by never reading out loud, tone deaf in a rhythmic sort of way. It eventually occurs to me that the differences might be the result of my own mistakes. Who sang the rhymes to me in the first place? My parents? Teachers at school? *Listen with Mother?* I have no recollection. I just seem to know the words. It's possible that I misheard them or changed them in my head, and then repeated the new version to my own children without reading the books properly. Perhaps this doesn't matter at all and nursery rhymes are meant to be transient, variations on a theme. Although I'm still puzzled about the ones that don't scan. They really don't work without rhythm.

There are sixty nursery rhymes altogether in the Ladybird series, twenty in each, and every page is crowded with cheerful images. On the cover of Book One, Little Bo Peep, dressed as a shepherdess (apparently based on the china figurines that old ladies used to keep in their glass-fronted, dark-wood cabinets), is peering into the distance from under her flowery bonnet, ignoring the sheep behind her; in the foreground, Humpty-Dumpty (in the uniform of a soldier) seems to have survived his fall and looks confused; next to him, a moustachioed dish is running away with the spoon, carrying a suitcase and looking hopeful; and a boy on a toy horse is heading for Banbury Cross in the background. Not bad for one cover.

I start to wonder why it's always considered necessary to illustrate the people in nursery rhymes with clothes and backgrounds from the past. Is everyone (including, apparently, children) yearning for a long-gone idyll where world annihilation had not yet been invented; a kind of golden age where women were plump and wore bonnets and had rosy cheeks, where girls had blonde ringlets and boys were dressed in lace collars and buckled shoes? Are the Victorians, apparently the inventors of childhood, whispering to us still? And why is Humpty-Dumpty always portrayed as an egg? There's nothing in the rhyme to suggest anything more than a fatal accident. Does Lewis Carroll have something to do with this?

It's hard to pinpoint a specific period that is being represented in the Ladybird series – it's not at all consistent. 'Peter, Peter, pumpkin eater,/ Had a wife and couldn't keep her' has a medieval feel (something to do with the hats), but why does 'As I was going to St Ives,/ I met a man with seven wives' (which incidentally, I wouldn't have identified as a nursery rhyme, more an old-fashioned riddle) have a carful of Barbie doll look-alikes, all seven of them dressed as if they've come straight out of 1950s Hollywood? It's a curious picture, this one, with them all piled into an early twentieth-century car. One of the wives is playing with kittens on a canopy above the car while a man on a bicycle, a guitar on his back, challenges them. How did all this find its way into a tale about a journey to Cornwall? But Yankee Doodle (should this really have a place in a book of English nursery rhymes?) has all the right gear for a frontiersman – beaver hat, musket, British soldiers in the background – which dates it fairly accurately to the American War of Independence.

It has to be said that not all the pictures are satisfactory. Little Polly Flinders warming her pretty little toes and ruining her nice new clothes, is endearing, whereas the image of Dr Foster falling into a puddle – a big fat man with a caved-in top hat, crossed eyes and enormous whiskers – is unlikely to induce a cosy glow of nostalgia in anyone who goes out in the rain, visits Gloucester or combines both activities. It's more frightening than reassuring, despite its snappy rhythm. And what about the creepy man in 'Goosey Goosey Gander', wandering upstairs and downstairs and in my lady's chamber, refusing to say his prayers? Are we supposed to cheer as we witness his head-first tumble over the banisters? Don't we advocate fair trials any more? Is there sufficient evidence to prove his guilt?

There are one or two that are less familiar: 'The man in the moon came down too soon/ and asked his way to Norwich./ He went by the south and burnt his mouth/ by eating cold plum porridge.' I wonder why he's wearing flying goggles. It's not as if they'd be much use once he left the atmosphere. But then he has apparently drifted down in a balloon. A certain lack of scientific expertise there, I would say. Although that could be the point. Reality is only for grown-ups.

> There was an old woman tossed up in a basket,
> Seventeen times as high as the moon;
> Where she was going I couldn't but ask her,
> For in her hand she carried a broom.
> Old woman, old woman, old woman, quoth I,
> Where are you going to up so high?
> To brush the cobwebs off the sky!
> May I go with you?
> Yes, by and by.

I like this one but can't explain why the image of a woman brushing cobwebs off the sky pleases me more than an unlikely astronaut who's worrying about his breakfast. It can't be the pictures. The man in the moon is distinctly odd, but the woman with the broom has a very alarmed child with her and her smile is deeply sinister. I'm not sure that it matters. Despite their oddness, the pictures bring back the words, demand that I chant them out loud.

I've heard, many times, that there's a deeper meaning to these rhymes. 'Ring-a-Ring-a-Roses', for example, was thought to have originated with the Black Death. It seems, however, that not everyone agrees with this interpretation and folklorists no longer attach significance to the words. I'm with them on this. These are not like fairy tales, dark and sinister, grappling with good and evil. Most of them are simple tales invented by ordinary people who wanted to introduce some fun into their lives. I like the idea of parents, grandparents, an uncle crippled with arthritis who live in a crooked house, sitting with their little ones and watching the world go by, finding a nice phrase, repeating it, establishing a rhythm and spinning it all into a neat little rhyme. 'Jack be nimble, Jack be quick, Jack jump over the candlestick.' Say the words out loud, click your fingers. It has a rhythm and it has a beat. Do we care if it doesn't mean anything?

So are these Ladybird books works of art or clumsy renditions that have no serious research behind them? Now that I've studied the pictures more closely, I have to conclude that they are not the work of an unacknowledged genius. Like the words, they are little more than gentle nonsense. Some are executed crudely (especially the ones with soldiers or sailors, and there are quite a few of those), but who can resist Little Jumping Joan, all alone, high in the air, mid-jump, her hair flying out behind her, caught in a stage spotlight? The lack of historical consistency is unnerving but probably irrelevant because they do their job. They place themselves in our memories.

So the words and the images are harmless but somehow significant in the process of growing up. We're familiar with the physical evidence of heritage, rooted in landscape and buildings, watched over by organizations like the National Trust, but we must remember to preserve our personal memories too, the experience of childhood that links us to long-gone generations. Our world seems to be shifting into a faster gear, whizzing past landmarks before we can see them clearly, moving on to the next wonder. There's no appetite for spare parts any more, mending or making do, no time to sit and look backwards while playing with words. Are we losing our sense of permanence? We shouldn't allow ourselves to become like those three blind mice, unaware as the farmer's wife creeps up behind them with her carving knife. Let's keep our tails intact, protect them, keep them safe.

CLARE MORRALL is a novelist and music teacher who lives in Birmingham. The most recent of her eight novels is *The Last of the Greenwoods*. Nursery rhymes play a significant part in her seventh novel, *When the Floods Came*.

Bibliography

Coming attractions

PAULINE MELVILLE decides she'd rather not · MICK HERRON
sees life on Cannery Row · CLIVE UNGER-HAMILTON develops
a taste for Paris · SARAH CROWDEN follows two middle-aged
ladies to Andalusia · RICHARD CROCKATT scales an Everest
of a book · MARGARET DRABBLE swims with the Water
Babies · ANTHONY GARDNER meets an irresistible cad ·
ANNABEL WALKER changes her mind about Cornwall ·
CHRIS SCHULER turns out his grandmother's attic

The *Slightly Foxed* Crossword No. 11: Answers

Across: 1 UNPOCKETED 6 ACOL 10 PETER 11 INFLICTED 12 THERESA
13 ERASMUS 14 RIDER HAGGARD 18 CROSS CHANNEL 21 ARBLAST
23 INGRAMS 24 *see 7 down* 25 ORGAN 26 SKYE 27 GREAT SCOTT

Down: 1 UPPITY 2 *see 7 down* 3 CORNELIUS BARRY 4 ELIZABETH 5 EFFIE
7 CATSMEAT POTTER PIRBRIGHT 8 LED ASIDE 9 HIRAM GREWGIOUS
15 HENRIETTA 16 ECHAPPES 17 DOGBERRY 19 DAGGOO 20 ASK NOT
22 TIGER